HORTICULTURAL HABITS:
A GARDENER'S JOURNEY

Acknowledgments

*I wish to thank all those in my personal life that
made this book possible.*

Mr. Nick Productions, LLC

Copy Editor – R. Graham

Front cover art – Dr. Mayputz and Fifteen Blue Design
Back cover and spine – Dr. Mayputz and Fifteen Blue Design
Book layout – Kristy Klein / FifteenBlue.com

Photo of alleged gardener – Anonymous
Published by Mr. Nick Productions, LLC ©2024

*TRIGGER WARNING –
This book contains words that may trigger laughter*

**This book was NOT written using
Artificial Intelligence or a ghostwriter**

ISBN: 979-8-218-38235-3

Dedications

To my departed paternal grandfather, Peter, or Petro as he
was called before emigrating to America. His
entrepreneurial agricultural wisdom and gardening skills
from the "old country" were somehow passed on to me. My
relationship with all plants, especially edible ones, eventually
blossomed into a steadfast partnership involving more love
than hate. Thank you, Grandpa.

To my adult daughter, and now young mother, Brigette.
You seem to have successfully embodied my zeal and
abilities for growing plants. Your green thumb is showing!

Horticulture, agriculture, gardening, oh my! Are they all one and the same or slightly different iterations of the same thing: namely, sticking seeds into the ground, growing them, and then consuming the resultant adult produce? Most likely, but the breadth and scope of the processes vary. Agriculture is basically large-scale farming, which includes raising trees and animals. Harvested plants can be fruits, fungi, veggies, flowers, and grasses that humans purposely grow for themselves, other people, and as feed for livestock. Botanical horticulture is scientific, small-scale cultivation of plants and includes dealing with gardening. Obviously, there are gobs of professionally written books available which are virtual plant "bibles"; ones that seek to answer questions such as how, when, where, and why to grow things. However, while not a professional, please join me as I try to explain

a lifetime journey of horticultural trials and tribulations involving my big backyard, vegetable plot, and beloved berry patches.

This is not my first bout in the sacred squared circle of the writing realm. Some readers may have already indulged in my previous comic literary offerings and hopefully found them enjoyable. This book is based on true events that continually transpire as I perspire while working in and around my garden. It also contains a host of obtuse observations and sometimes-twisted gardening conclusions. As an aside, no plants were purposely harmed except for those eaten during the writing process. This is a book of humor and should be taken as such. There is no malicious intent; the only intent is to entertain!

Dr. I. Mayputz
I identify as someone who is offended by
offensive people, myself included!

Table of Contents

Introduction

How can seasonal gardening, landscape maintenance, and growing more than a few berry bushes simultaneously be a psychological bane and balm? The contrast seems especially odd for someone who has dabbled extensively in horticulture for decades. Yet it's so true. Much like that addictive and daft sport called pickleball, a leisurely and seemingly *healthy* "putter in the garden" can become an all-consuming lifestyle. However, I'm not talking about authentic farmers or Amish folk, for whom toiling in the soil is both vocation and sustenance. No, I'm speaking of the white-collar professional who, although ambivalent toward self-grown edible plants as a youth, now fancies himself a fervent grower of fruits and veggies. One who becomes frequently frustrated and obsessed with results instead of appreciating the physical and mental benefits of "the growing process." Fresh berries and vegetables are fine, but it's the body and mind that benefit the most from digging in the dirt! Anyway, let's dig in and explore these plant-based, juxtapositional tales. And as always, most names and places have been altered so as not to overtly embarrass anyone, plants included. Hopefully you will find the stories within the following pages to be humorous and you will laugh along with me. Maybe at me as well!

1

Always a Farmer

I was born in a large, industrialized, city in western New York State. Dad was employed as a professional civil engineer by an architectural firm and Mom was a stay-at-home housewife (she became a much beloved French and Spanish-teaching college professor much later in life). But there were more people in our cramped household, namely my foreign-born paternal grandparents. Grandpa Pete was a persecuted victim of Stalinist pogroms in the 1930's which were directed against non-communist aristocratic agronomists (well-off landowners and estate-farmers) who employed peasants. The sorry story of Grandpa's young and middle-aged life cannot be overstated. Then WWII carnage got in the way, as well. There were plenty of ways that death could have come for him, his wife, and his only child (my father) as they zigzagged through war-torn Europe, but they escaped to the supposed "Promised Land" of E pluribus unum as legitimate and duly naturalized Displaced Persons. Although starting off rough and without a strong command of the English language, my highly intelligent and sporty father married a gal who was also from the "home country," and together with his parents moved into a dinky two-story house on Mills

Street. Pop had earlier graduated from a vaunted U. S. college and gained steady employment while Grandpa Pete toiled away in a local tool-and-die factory. At the same time, Mom and her kerchief-wearing mother-in-law tended to the aqua-colored, non-descript house. There was also a twenty-square-foot grassy backyard complete with a large pear tree in the middle of it. A few trimmed hedges lined the street-side front and the length of the narrow driveway. Oh, and there was a used but immaculate '51 gray Delta 88 Oldsmobile parked in the smallish garage. But there was no arable land or wherewithal for growing edible plants. Working hard, making money and surviving was the credo and impetus of most hard-working European transplants in those bygone days. And my folks were no exception. Their eventual monetary advantage over most American natives was part of the "immigrant" mindset and extended family group dynamic: two males working and two females taking care of things at home, thereby pooling together resources and saving the meager, moola that was earned. However, there was a new mouth to feed; a male child was born in 1959 – me. But no worries, enough money was available to feed all of us. And there was always the local Broadway Market to go to. It was a huge indoor and outdoor emporium catering largely to former Europeans. Delectable fresh veggies, meats, fish, sausages, candies, pastries, breads, etc. were always for sale. But besides picking the free pears in the backyard every fall, we did not dig in the dirt and plant things. However, my young life was about to change in a hurry! There were personal grumblings at home and general unhappiness with the hustle-bustle of city life. Dad desperately wanted a change from the city rat race and Mom needed to escape from her domineering father-in-law, who still fancied himself as a Hetman (ancient Slavic tribal chief). Plus, my folks didn't want me growing up as a street-smart city *urchin*. So, Pop metaphorically shed his old stripes as a slide-rule wielding *mensch* and reinvented himself as a slide-rule instructing professor in a puny, Ag and Tech college located in a dusty, no-account village in southeastern New York State. It was in the middle of sparsely populated hill country, and about a five-hour drive away from my now-widowed grandfather. I reluctantly began kindergarten as the darkest kid in my class, my dad enthusiastically began teaching civil engineering to college students, and my elated mom felt liberated to be out from under the thumb of her bossy father-in-law. All was bliss, although the euphoric feelings only lasted for a limited number of years. Grandpa Pete retired from work, sold the old house, packed his belongings, carpet-bagged-it due east in his Oldsmobile, and unceremoniously *plotzed* in our tiny rental house on Clinton Street. Family was still family; he had gotten lonely and had nowhere else to go. Oh well, it HAD been a good ride while it lasted. Unfortunately, the same slightly dysfunctional family dynamic was rekindled, with Grandpa Pete as the self-appointed head of the table, so to speak. But there was one difference this time around. There were plans to build a brand-new house on a quarter acre of purchased land on a dead-end road near the outskirts of our "bovine-infested" settlement. That thought alone kept peace in the home. Meanwhile, I was becoming somewhat of a bug-hunter and had permission to scour the backyards and multiple gardens of elderly neighbors to my heart's content. I loved chasing and catching butterflies and other insects. Salamander sleuthing at a nearby brook was my other zoological pastime during the summers of the late '60s and early '70s. However, before Dad had designed and drawn up the final blueprints for our new home, the sloped plot of land was carefully scrutinized by Grandpa Pete. And his former agrarian roots would not let him off the hook. It's as if all those years living in a dirty and crowded American city did not matter - he was still a "farmer" deep down inside. And here was a large patch of living, breathing soil that he could once again harness to do his bidding. Besides, why fight with my mom when he could fight with plants? During the year prior to our large house being built (by he and my pop), he requisitioned a small square of cleared ground, plowed a few small rows, and sowed some seeds as a "test" garden. But the soil in the Catskills was much different from the rich black topsoil of the "old country," or even from the soil found in the filthy U.S. city from whence he had recently moved. He was concerned about the amethyst-hued and very rocky disposition of the "new" ground and grew disenchanted. "How can anything grow in this crappy, red-colored and stone-filled mud?" he bitterly bellowed in Estonian one evening at dinner. "It is sickly sludge, nothing will sprout," he further lamented. "But other village idiots have nice gardens," my mother sarcastically interjected as she fed my toddler baby sister. "That's right. Why don't you visit some of our future neighbors on the hill and check out what they are growing," my dad added. Grandpa Pete did just that and in very broken English managed to communicate and then elucidate some tips and tricks from the local, *homeboy* gardeners in his newly adopted mountain town. His resultant and seemingly futile attempt at gardening in supposedly subpar conditions paid dividends. Not only did plants spring out, but vegetables actually grew well in this god-forsaken and seemingly "lifeless" loam. He was very pleased and could not wait to begin a humongous garden after our house was completed. He imagined it would sit on a properly plowed and weed-free plot in the raised terrace behind our house. His imagination was spot-on as the idea came to fruition. Little did I know that it would not be long before my sister and I would be coerced, cajoled, and browbeaten into unwilling farmhands, all to satisfy the whims of an old but spirited man whose dormant gardening genes finally became expressed again. In the summers I had to literally get on my bike and ride away or sneakily leave unnoticed to hunt "bugs and slugs." Otherwise, I would be unwillingly corralled, conscripted, and commandeered for hours-long "garden duty." There was always something that needed watering, hoeing, rocks that needed to be removed, destructive potato beetle larvae picked off, etc. I started to hate that yearly garden. And then there were also red raspberries and currants to pick. Holy hell, when could my sister and I be kids and have fun? This was America, not Estonia where the agriculturally raised youngsters of yesteryear were basically free child labor! And don't get me started on the harvesting season. Grandpa Pete's whole psyche became entwined in that damn piece of land that he grew fruits and vegetables on, just like in the old days when he was a workaholic and strapping young lad. Of course, I am embellishing a bit, but not much. Nevertheless, there were also many happy summer moments with my father, mother, and sister involving swimming, tennis, camping, fishing, hunting, and doing the odd projects around the yard and house. My grandfather would rarely but sometimes join us during those precious family-oriented outings. He didn't have his nose in the sod 24/7. Though with his trusty slingshot in hand, he would often sit in his opened and shady little green shed for hours on end while gazing over his dominion and watching my sister and I slave away in the hot sun. Perhaps it reminded him somewhat of his original gigantic Estonian plantation, from which he was forcibly evicted. Maybe it was also a psychological respite after having suffered through a tumultuous early life. No matter what the reason, I noticed his behavior and was determined NOT to end up like him. No way Jose', although…. In summary, my distant discordant memories of gardening are often more vividly recalled than pleasant ones. Yet, something about planting, raising and eating bounty from the earth had made an indelible mental mark on me just the same. And that's how my love/hate relationship with amateur, home-based horticulture began.

2

Gardens Galore

As a very young lad, traipsing around unsupervised behind the homes of kindly widows on stately Clinton Street was wonderful. It was the boulevard where we initially lived on rent as a family before our large house was built nearby. As a "natural-born" naturalist and amateur entomologist, I was constantly stepping around gardens in the backyards of the nice folks that allowed me to trespass. They trusted a precocious youngster with a butterfly net in hand to run hither thither between planted beds of flowers and veggies, all in the pursuit of moths, butterflies, and other insects. But I kept my non-verbalized promise not to damage or even slightly disturb any growing plant that I happened to jump over or quickly sidestep when trying to catch Tiger Swallowtails and Monarchs. The elderly retirees probably delighted in watching me during my naturalistic endeavors and I delighted in usually getting my quarry. Even when I moved into my new home, I still visited Clinton Street to get my fill of aerial critters. But it was the subliminal exposure to horticultural habits that most likely "sowed the seeds" in my mind, namely that growing gardens were natural and normal pastimes. Nearly every backyard I traversed had one. Large, small, whatever - they were ubiquitous and lovingly cared for. And this was the late '60s and early '70s, before "organic" and "natural" became common buzzwords for healthy eating and living. People just had fruit and vegetable plots as part of their spring/summer lifestyles. Of course, all the dairy farmers surrounding our puny settlement had gardens, but veggie plots were not really necessary for most of the Village People. We had two supermarkets and a few mom-and-pop food emporiums in our desolate dump. However, perhaps something in the Depression-era mindsets of the still-living oldsters compelled them to grow their own food and maybe save a few sawbucks in the process? Who knows? All I knew was that households having a stretch of dirt with plants growing out of it every summer was the norm in our backward backwater. And though my grandfather's relatively new garden-planning scheme was taking root and quickly becoming a family obsession, I willingly accepted it. Was it "green brainwashing"? I don't know. How can you truly hate growing plants when nearly everyone around us was gardening, and seemingly loving it? I was needlessly excited; what a dummy I was.

3

Go Big or Go Home

Our new house was recently completed on a quarter acre of hilly, terraced land. My live-in Grandpa Pete, who extensively helped my father build the home, was just itching to start tilling the dirt for real. He had previously experimented by planting a few rows of veggies the year before and was surprised, yet pleased with the results. Even though the "slack soil," as he insultingly called it in his native Estonian, was rocky and purple-colored, he managed to wrangle some decent lettuce, beets and beans from it. Now he was all excited to escalate his endeavors. A huge rototiller was purchased, the flat terrace behind our house was eyeballed as the "garden mecca," and the work soon began. Curiously, Pop was lukewarm and Mom ambivalent about all things agricultural. Sure, they ate their greens, but the thought of veggie self-sufficiency including planting, growing, harvesting, canning, and freezing was not on their hit list. But it was on Grandpa Pete's! Somehow, he managed to convince the family that fresh fruits and vegetables were well worth the cost of our minimal participation and labor. Of course, Mom and Dad were ecstatic that he had an all-consuming summer pastime, leaving them alone. Well, that really did not happen, especially for my sister and me. Planning for the garden, starting seedlings in containers in April, and buying seeds were constant topics of conversation every spring that I grew weary of. But Mom would often say, "Hey, if it makes the grumpy old man happy, why not?" His caustic belligerence and old-world, rough-cut customs did not exactly fit into Americana, but, hey, growing a benign garden might be a soothing tonic for him. And it was, sort of. But what a process it turned out to be. Not content to let his local-yokel neighbors outshine him and his Estonian farming wisdom, Grandpa decided to use every spare inch of plowable land that he could. Pop came home from teaching one day in early May and stared at the rototilled area, which took Grandpa all day to do. "Is he planning on feeding the entire town?" Dad remarked, with a concerned look on his face. "I don't know. He's been at it without a break for the entire day," Mom sullenly muttered. And remember, Grandpa Pete was not a young man. However, he was fit as a fiddle and resembled an elite Master's athlete, although he had never run, nor had he caught or kicked a ball in his life. Great genetics, I guess. Anyway, the humungous plot was prepared, and Grandpa announced his grandiose plans for planting and plans for us mere mortals living in the same house as him. Oh no. Somehow, I knew it would involve us. He then blurted out that if we wanted to eat, we had to pitch in. What? How did this happen? How did we survive before? Mom would go shopping at Grand Union and my father never cried bankruptcy. And wasn't this whole thing supposed to be HIS big idea? Since when did it become OUR collective hobby? Was he going to buy farm animals next? How did we get roped into this mess? I was mad as hell but tried not to show it. He also wanted Pop to buy an extra freezer for all the planned produce that would be picked and frozen. Dad gave in, bought the freezer chest and sort of promised that my sister, Mom, and I would be involved in Grandpa's over-the-top horticultural dalliance. Thanks a lot, Pop! Of course, Dad disappeared at every cotton-picking opportunity to pursue tennis with his buddies, go target shooting with the local pistol team, or fix watches in his private home lair (he was a brilliant amateur horologist). So that left Mom, my sister, and me as unwilling servants at the "General's" beck and call to "assist" him with gardening duties. It was so unfair, I tell you. And now on to the growing aspects. That first gigantic garden and subsequent ones were indeed huge and included most vegetables in neatly spaced subplots, measured rows, and rectangular patches. Corn, Russian (American Oxheart) tomatoes, rhubarb, strawberries, carrots, peas, beans, squash, beets, etc. were planted, religiously weeded, watered, and tenderly tended to.

And not to mention the endless rows of currants, red raspberries, and fruit trees that were planted and then induced to do Grandpa Pete's bidding. It was certainly a lot of plant life to be suddenly responsible for. The new neighbors' initial gardening camaraderie, frequent kibitzing and jovial natures turned to envy, silence, and bitterness when they witnessed the successful "Titanic of gardens" in their midst. Most did not realize that my grandfather was an old-school Estonian farmer at heart, had previously owned and operated a vast agrarian estate, and absolutely and resolutely knew his way around a hoe, sickle, spade, and rake! The local roughnecks were pissed, my sister and I were frequently overwhelmed with all the work we had to do, yet Grandpa Pete smugly smiled whenever he inspected his vegetative "baby." Anyway, even though I resented that damn garden on most sunny days, I recall thinking about the hearty, organically raised fruits and veggies I dined on. I remember that our produced produce tasted much better than identical veggies bought from the Victory supermarket in our Podunk village. However, I was also frequently steamed for having to duck and swerve out of Grandpa Pete's sight on many summer mornings to do my own "thing." In hindsight I feel that the importance of horticultural pursuits somehow became ingrained in me, whether through genetics or from my grandfather's endless derogatory diatribes directed at me for being a derelict and directionless young man. Perhaps in a weird way I am psychologically showing him how responsible I am by taking care of my family and other living things, green ones at that. Either way, gardening stuck with me, and I still have a *relationship* with plants.

4

Slingshot Diplomacy

Unlike Henry Kissinger and his clandestine shuttle diplomacy initiatives under President Nixon during the mid '70s, Grandpa Pete's idea of settling differences in his vast garden was through force, namely using the slingshot. Besides, the various birds and mammalian varmints did not understand language, only slung stones that stung. Nary a pest got the best of my grandfather, no way. Similar to fictional Mr. McGregor and his offensive approach to uninvited and unwanted veggie-moochers, Grandpa was always prepared to do battle with his own weapon of choice: a trusty handmade slingshot. And I was usually there observing him when he carefully selected a small, forked wooden branch as if part of a holy springtime ritual. He sawed, sanded and polished the custom-made appliance. Then he lovingly fastened two separate thick rubber bands - complete with a tied-on leather pocket between them - onto the wooden contraption and voila', he was finished. And ready to minister to the many miscreants that sought to chow down in his beloved garden. Ordinarily, he wasn't a violent man, but something about protecting his turf and family brought out the "toxic" male in him. And forget about purchasing a store-bought slingshot. He made his own, just like he used to as a young lad. However, he didn't use lethal steel shot as ammunition, only small, rounded stones. Actually, he did not really want to kill anything; his "shooting" was merely as a deterrent. And I knew he was telling the truth. I witnessed him aiming on a few occasions and accurately hitting unwary woodchucks and rabbits squarely in their respective keesters making them jump up and take painful notice. His aim could be deadly, but the results were seldom such. Most of the time, he discharged his "stones" in the general direction of the derelict animal in question, just to send a message of warning and to make it leave. But they never learned of course, making his near-daily presence important. As stated, my sister and I were frequently browbeaten into summertime involuntary "serfdom" to tend to the garden as needed. While we were toiling away weeding or something, stones periodically whizzed over our heads, or landed next to us if some rascally rodents or avian marauders were nearby. Fortunately, neither my sister nor I lost a tooth, an eye or even got hit. Lucky us. Thank goodness Grandpa was an expert marksman. And although I admired and appreciated his expert workmanship and ultimate usage of the slingshot, I never gravitated to having one. Unlike Luke Skywalker, I never made my own lightsaber, I mean slingshot. I'm sure Gramps would have gladly made one for me had I only asked. But I never did. Something about pulling back rubber bands that could possibly snap off and hit you in the face did not appeal to me. It did not happen to Grandpa Pete, but easily could have. Anyhow, as an adult, Hav-A-Hart traps, chicken wire fencing, netting, and my trusty, un-scoped, pump-action, pellet rifle are some of the tools I currently use to successfully maintain "humane" and human dominance in the never-ending critter-battles concerning coveted fruits and veggies. Well, at least over creatures that are larger than insects.

5

Destructive Insect Pests

In addition to the aforementioned rodents and birds that plague most every garden at some point or another, there are certain six-legged arthropods and their voracious juvenile delinquents to contend with as well. The larval stages of insects can be more destructive than the adults, munching feverishly on selective vegetable matter prior to pupating. Although Grandpa Pete could have easily purchased and applied popular and potent insecticides such as Rotenone, he did not. Hell, DDT was legal to use up until 1972! No, thanks to my sister and me, we had an "organic" and "natural" garden without even knowing what those words meant at the time. I'm not sure what kind of insecticides were used "down on the farm" in old Estonia, if any, but Grandpa saw no value in using them in his new garden in the Catskills. Neem oil, Garlic oil, dish washing detergent, tobacco extract, as well as home-made "tonics and elixirs" could have been used as organic pest controls. Alas, Grandpa Pete did not seem to believe in ANY chemical intervention when it came to quelling the persistent pestilence involving our garden because he had my sister and I as two able-bodied "helpers." Our task was to pick off the destructive slugs, bugs, aphids, potato beetles and their larvae, Cabbage Butterfly eggs and their caterpillars that hid inside inner cabbage leaves, Armyworms on corn, etc. We were each issued a small container and tiny pointed stick and told to go through the various rows, without stepping on any plants, and physically collect ANY destructive little demons which would then be disposed of. I love entomology, but even I have to agree that some insects are not the gardener's friends. I resentfully saw the value of our work. Without a grunt or peep, my little sister would put her head down and do what she was told, knowing full well that after a few hours we would be "free," even to go swimming at the village pool that Mom would take us to. That was the reward on very hot summer days (of course very hot in those days meant barely breaking 80 degrees F.). Sis never complained and seemed to have a stoic attitude about the arduous labor. She was a good soldier. As her older brother, I was the one carping and chafing at the bit to quickly get things over with and then possibly go swimming. Grandpa Pete would examine our *creepy-crawly* filled buckets, begrudgingly collect them, and then summarily dismiss us. No gratitude, no nothing. And we were his *beloved* and ONLY grandkids! I quickly figured out that WE were the human insecticides that kept things growing, darn it. But I expected as much from an old-school, old-fashioned, and traditional farmer who most likely treated family members worse than his former hired hands. I never received ANY praise or even a *shekel* for my summertime efforts wiling away in the dirt at his behest. It was unnecessary in his book. After all, my sister and I were family, effective and worked cheaply. What was not to love?

6

That's Quite Enough!

While visiting my elderly folks at my boyhood home one day, I chanced to walk up to the flat, terraced area behind the house and took in the green grass growing there. That *hallowed* ground had been our humongous garden of yesteryear. "Had been" are the operative words. From 1969 to 1992, that piece of acreage was my paternal Grandpa Pete's sacred place. It was simultaneously his bane and a source of solace. Using old-school, Estonian-gleaned agricultural knowledge, he managed to wrangle a constant supply of fruits and vegetables for our lunch and dinner tables. After a stroke felled him at age 92 in 1992 – though he did not pass until seven years later – my dad "took over" the major horticultural chores of running that oversized garden plot. Mom helped out as she always did, however, my sister and I were long gone from that household. It became just the two of them working that parcel of land. Both felt morally obligated to continue what Grandpa had started and to honor his memory at the same time. Plus, they got great fruity and veggie yields. But it was a lot of effort. He had maintained it as a fulltime job/hobby whereas my folks did not. I heard there were petty squabbles betwixt them as to whose turn it was to hill the potato plants or do the weeding between the rows of lettuce, etc. And remember, both parents were newly retired former professors with plenty of retirement income and did not need the stress and aggravation of a garden to supplement them with foodstuffs. They could easily afford as much grub as desired and plainly did not need the headaches of a big garden. Sure, the supermarket produce was not as organic or fresh, but so what? It was time to wind down. They also scaled back on the regular purchases of naturally raised beef, pork, milk and eggs from local farmers in the area. In other words, although they were not outwardly physically infirm, it seems as though my folks finally shed their old "Amish" ways and acquiesced to spending more time and money on travel, leisure activities, and sports. Both were avid tennis players and had a local posse of like-minded peeps that they played with. Especially my aged father, who was still able to play doubles at a very high level (being a former college tennis coach didn't hurt). So, the garden started to take a back seat to my folks' newfound freedom and desires in retirement. And as my mother related to me, one fall day in 1999, after the garden was put to bed, Pop looked out the back window and pronounced to no one in particular, "That's quite enough." But Mom heard him loud and clear. And that was it; he had spoken the unvarnished and drawn-out truth at last. It was high time to stop the madness and stop gardening! Mom was as relieved as he, it seems. Dad bought more than a few large bags of grass seed, liberally broadcast the contents onto the now-barren landscape, raked it in, and he was done. The next spring a different greenery emerged from that field. Friends and neighbors came 'round and congratulated them on finally stopping that all-consuming endeavor. Although a few apple trees, currant-berry shrubs, and raspberry bushes remained, the ensuing spring, summer, and autumn seasons would be without the toil required of playing "Farmer in the Dell." My sister and I were shocked at first but then thought about how much time and effort our own gardens sucked out of us. Years passed and all Pop did was periodically mow that formerly magical area with his lawn tractor. As I paused to stare at that neatly mowed section I recalled all the rocks my sis and I had formerly picked out of there, the potato beetle larvae we picked off the potato leaves, the hot and sweaty days when we picked ripe berries…. Pick, pick, pick - I "hated" that garden as a youth but had no idea that my father despised it as well. Who knew? When it came time for him to literally take over the reins, he essentially abdicated. Initially, and for a few years, he halfheartedly continued the charade, but then dumped it like a psycho girlfriend. Maybe he was right to do that. I don't know. I continued to gaze at that smoothly coifed terrace and thought about MY small garden and berry plots. They still brought me joy and more than a few berries and vegetables, right? Right? I guess, as the strangely fond horticultural remembrances of my childhood comingled with outright anger. Mixed emotions ensued although reminiscing brought about a certain degree of satisfaction. The clouded memories weren't all bad. There were many good times, like when we shelled peas on the front porch while talking and laughing as a family unit. And when we enthusiastically dug up baskets of potatoes or shucked bushels of corn while grinning from ear to ear. Nostalgia can be a vacillating bitch depending on new perceptions of old realities.

7

Maintenance

That one word often conjures up thoughts of keeping the status quo. Preservation, conservation, and constantly greasing the skids would be other words and phrases to use. But it's such an important noun when it comes to raising edible plants, and gardeners predisposed to being of a certain micromanaging nature seem to fare better than others when toiling in the soil. Letting the garden grow without observation and active involvement - such as weeding, fertilizing, pruning, mulching, watering, trellising, insect and varmint-busting - are recipes for a resultant poor harvest. Unfortunately, I have seen this disastrous scenario play out firsthand while visiting various family members and listening to their respective gripes about gardening. For many beginners, the most fun happens during the scheming, seeding and sowing stages. However, the roll-up-your-sleeves and hoe-in-the-hot-sun phase is frequently downplayed or omitted, and then the whole damn veggie plot goes to pot. Well, not to pot unless you are growing Mary Jane on purpose. You get my drift. Like raising a child, you can't quit after it is born and still hope for a positive outcome. The same basic principles apply to gardening, I'm afraid.

Don't plan and undertake building a slew of raised beds if you are not fully committed to MAINTAINING them - wood rots and steel rusts. Of course, you can always hire help, etc. However, for the SMALLTIME amateur, I suggest starting SMALL and staying SMALL. Unless family members are self-motivated or coerced into helping out, going solo can be a daunting task. My long-retired and physically fit paternal grandfather, who lived with my family when I was growing up, made his humongous garden a daily obsession for three quarters of the year. But that's hardly normal and not for everyone. And even HE made my sister and I chip in with horticultural chores as needed. Anyhow, today our very small vegetable garden and berry patches are just what my wife and I can handle. And as we ungracefully age and become more decrepit, we are grateful that we never felt inclined to expand the plots and become a true "farming family." Sure, we have available acreage, but no thank you. It would just be too much work for the two of us. Backyard veggie gardening and fruit-growing, much like pickleball, is supposed to be productive and fun, with the emphasis on FUN. Otherwise, why do it? Unless lots of harvested food is necessary to augment a meager lifestyle, the casual suburban gardener can get plenty of psychological satisfaction AND fresh veggies from a smallish, manageable garden. So, beware the allure of the seed catalogs that still come in the mail with glossy photos of gorgeous produce on the pages. Take it from a dilapidated, and possibly canceled, dirty old coot: No one prefers cisgender, binary, straight, *hot*, blue-eyed, blonde-haired women more than me, but I continue to only stick with my wife Hottie Blondie. The same goes for gardening, specifically: don't bite off more than you can chew.

Three Sheds

As the flatbed truck slowly trundled out of our big backyard, after unceremoniously dumping a small, 6 x 8-foot, Amish-built wooden shed next to and in line with two larger ones, my wise-cracking daughter piped up. "Gee, Dad, I didn't know you were competing with Arthur 'Two Sheds' Jackson," she laughed out loud. I also chuckled while instantly remembering that name and certain hilarious sketch from the zany members of Monty Python's Flying Circus. My teenage daughter was a chip off the old blockhead and, besides having a mutual fondness for all things creepy-crawly, we both still share a love of irreverent comedy. She and I will often quote seminal lines from The Three Stooges back and forth as well as enunciate the quirky and witty banter from Marx Brothers films, Abbott and Costello shorts, and the bawdy Benny Hill Show. Additionally, we also utter familiar funny phrases from circa '70s Monty Python TV shows and their subsequent movies. But back then, she was right. Now I had THREE sheds, one better than 'Two Sheds' Jackson and two more than my old Grandpa Pete. He only had one measly, self-built, green clapboard-sided shack. It was located next to his "victory garden" which was at the top of a terraced hill behind the home where I grew up. Anyway, I was the proud owner of a trifecta of sturdily constructed, shingled, vinyl-sided buildings to house the plethora of machinery that was deemed necessary to keep my backyard *wilderness* under control. The out-buildings – not outhouses – would also house ALL kinds of gardening implements and accoutrements to properly keep my berries and veggies growing, and me groaning. Gardening can be hard work with or without mechanical help. But were that many sheds really called for? Come on, I only had three acres of land on which to mow, sow and hoe. My berry patches were not that big, and neither was my veggie plot. Okay, so my lawn was large, but so what? Neighboring nosy neighbors had larger grassy tracts to cut and sculpt and they only had one shed apiece, at best. Well, as the next vignette will vividly illustrate, there was a method to my madness. Well, not to absolve my overall "madness," but at least I had a valid reason for accumulating so many expensive sheds.

9

Double or Nothing

To the casual observer, having three sheds means that I must have loads of various types of equipment and implements. But au contraire! Basically, I have DOUBLE of most everything, including traps, tractors, and tillers. But why? Why invest in a duplicative and expensive armamentarium when it will only be used for seasonal horticultural "pleasures"? Well, that is the point right there. Nothing makes me more frustrated than getting ready to mow and have my lawn tractor conk out on me. Or to have rake tines break or a shovel snap when needed most. Perhaps it is just me, but when I set out to do some supposedly fulfilling agricultural chores, I expect my tools to work. However, even though I meticulously take good care of them, "they" don't always reciprocate. Hence, buying double of everything usually allows me to continue on my merry gardening way without worrying that my push mower's carburetor just exploded or pruning shears fell apart. Like a fully loaded football team, it's always "next man up" when relied-upon inanimate objects suddenly go down in my yard. Of course, I will repair something myself if need be. However, I prefer to get the particular gardening chore done first before I roll up my sleeves and give aid to an ailing piece of machinery. But if I can't assuage a damaged item, I will call on my former dental patient, and technically retired small-engine repairman, who can get it back to me in working order for a very reasonable fee. He must still be grateful for the well-fitting dentures I made him long ago. But I hate to wait! While he is tinkering and tending to my stalled weed whacker, I pick up my other one and continue whacking off those ever-wandering weeds as needed. By now most of you may be thinking that I am a paranoid *nudnik*. And some of you may be partially correct in that assumption. But while churlish neighbors are busy cussing out failed equipment or getting greasy trying to repair their broken lot while nervously watching their grass grow ever taller, I am cheerfully riding along on my zero-turn lawn tractor even though my other one is in the shop. Everything tends toward entropy, meaning that everything gets disordered in life. Nothing fixes itself or gets better with age. Well, maybe fine wine and my wife, Hottie Blondie…. Anyway, since most things break down when you least expect them to, I buck Murphy's Law and am always ready to give it the proverbial finger. I don't care if my hoe breaks or if ceramic flowerpots crack over the winter. I have identical extras ready to fill the bill and "hold up their end of the bargain," so to speak. But the costly buying required to maintain a

vast arsenal of horticultural weaponry can be steep.
After all, gardening and yard maintenance are
purported to be soothing tonics for the white-collar
body and soul and not grueling and bank account-
draining endeavors. Right? And this "double or
nothing" sentiment applies to my home life in
general. No worries if my forced hot air fuel oil
furnace suddenly stops working when the
temperature drops to below zero outside. I have
enough brand-new belts, parts, and pieces to rebuild
TWO new furnace engines and blower fans if need
be. If my sump pumps cease sumping and pumping,
I have new ones at-the-ready to take their places in a
hurry, and so forth. Anyhow, when having a leisurely
putter in the garden, it's nice to slip on some leather
work gloves, notice holes in the fingers, and merrily
chuck them into the trash container knowing full well
that I have at least two additional pairs that are
willing and able to coat my hands for the day ahead.
And one more thing: most of my gardening and
lawnmowing aids are currently gasoline powered.
Only my leaf blower is lithium battery-operated and
rechargeable. Nevertheless, it more than "virtue
signals" the supposed oncoming *green* wave of the
immediate future. However, the inconvenient truth
of the distant future may be a tad dystopian: once the
world-wide, strip-mined lithium sources are depleted,
and Chinese-made lithium batteries become

non-existent or outrageously expensive, it will become a real challenge to keep "operating electrically." And with fossil fuels being relegated to the dustbin of history, will heretofore undiscovered, inexpensive, readily available and renewable energies step up and deliver? Let's hope so, because nuclear reactors, windmills, and solar panels have a long way to go before they can be miniaturized and strapped onto lawn tractors as power sources. Lol.

10

Master Gardener?

Wow, a Master Gardener at last. At least that's what the printed certificate read. It was the early nineties; my young family and I had recently moved into a newly built home (engineered and constructed by my father, grandfather, and a few contractors) on a three-acre parcel of land in the "country." Not really in the boonies, but not congested like true suburbs, either. A top tier public high school was within walking distance and the nearest grocery store, gas station, and pizza joint were a mere two miles away. I was the owner of a busy private dental practice in a nearby city, my wife was working as a part-time pharmacist at a local CVS, our two kids were in elementary school, and our first puny garden was an experiment patterned after my ginormous childhood one. I had learned a thing or three about home-grown horticulture from my old-fashioned and Estonian immigrant Grandpa Pete. Plus, I had lived the "gardening life" as a youth. I often cursed the rocks and berries I alternatively picked, not to mention the tedious and hot summer days that my sis and I had to endure while endlessly weeding. It was like a forced labor camp, with my sister and I being the chumps at the beck and call of my agriculturally addicted paternal grandfather. Anyway, now it was my turn as an adult to foist the same kind of vegetative trauma on my wife and children. Not quite. My liberal and progressive brats told me in no uncertain terms that they would be permanently "unavailable" for pedestrian, agrarian pursuits. "My younger brother and I are not Estonian peasants," my wiseacre daughter chortled. And she meant it. My steadfast wife said she would help but would not be unwillingly conscripted for garden duty. Sheesh, what a damn family! Just as an aside, both kids came out okay, if you can call it that. My daughter ended up earning a B.Sc. in Applied Zoology at McGill University and a highly coveted Ph.D. in entomology from the University of Connecticut. My son was the valedictorian of his prep school class and then graduated from Brown University and Duke Law School. Not bad for two non-serfs! I can't complain now, but at the time I was fuming mad. Well, it was all on my shoulders to wrestle eatable vittles from a smallish garden, some newly planted fruit trees and multiple berry bushes. And I reasoned that a Master Gardener's certificate would greatly help. However, I was only partially right about the whole experience. I had found out about the various Cornell Cooperative Extension departments, in local county seats that administer the Master Gardening courses, from a dental patient. After hearing her impassioned verbiage about it, I was determined to follow through on this supposedly substantive class. I hastily hired an available associate dentist to partially cover for me. Then I paid the paltry tuition, bought the required books and supplies, and enrolled whole hog in the ballyhooed all-day program. The weekly course was held on Mondays in a large hall complete with metal tables and uncomfortable fold-out steel chairs in a sprawling county complex of connected buildings. The venue was right next door to the gigantic, centralized, DMV office. Man, oh man, I was all set to learn how to properly plant, prune, and pick produce. How exciting. "Oh boy, is this great!" as Flounder of *Animal House* fame once said. And so, after perfunctory remarks by the so-called "higher ups" in the Extension office, the course began. It was composed of hired speakers, each with a specialty to share and passionately preach about. As I glanced around the large room, I noticed that the majority of attendees were women, or at least they physically identified as such. A few token *males*, including me, were also sporadically scattered among the motley mob. And everyone had pens and paper at the ready except for me. Why? This wasn't high school or college. There were no tests or quizzes or a final exam at the end. This was supposed to be a fun course. Weren't we there to soak up any additional horticultural knowledge that we didn't already know?

And that's what the reading materials were for: in case you missed a point in class, you could look it up later, right? I started to feel uneasy as I numbly sat there in the very back row, just like I had done in ALL of my pharmacy college and dental school classes. And just like college, there were the obligatory brown-noses and bootlickers sitting in the front row with winsome and knowing smiles on their faces. Some things never change; never mind that the ages of most of the adult students were over sixty-five apiece. I was probably one of the youngest ones present and keenly felt it from the elderly crowd. Nevertheless, I kept on showing up and kept on 'larnin. Most of the instructors were experts in their respective fields, and some were even local radio and television gardening celebrities. The classes were also full of slide presentations and overhead-projector-type lecturing. After eating homemade, bagged lunches, the afternoon sessions were much the same as the morning stints: more talking, more slides to gawk at, and sometimes a quick soporific siesta after the midday meal kicked in! The covered topics ranged from berry growing and proper pruning techniques to forest conservation and soil composition. It was a varied and eclectic mix of many agricultural subjects that I personally found interesting. The fourteen-week course ended, and we were all proclaimed Master Gardeners. Not horticulturists, which is designated as a professional title, but basically amateur gardeners with an official lifetime "license." Yippee, it sounded peachy keen. Kind of like being a juvenile member of the Smokey Bear Association or a Cub Scout. At the mandatory convocation, complete with food, drinks, and party favors, we lionized and feted graduates also received official pins and professional cards denoting our rarefied status in the gardening community, writ large. But hold up there, player. What was the real purpose of such unwarranted pomp and circumstance for a bunch of dumpy and frumpy seniors who recently learned a little something about tree trimming and root rot? Was there an ulterior motive involved? I quickly found out that new graduates were routinely browbeaten into voluntarily manning the phones in shifts at the agricultural section of the Extension office to field calls from the public. It was "expected" from ALL of the newly minted Master Gardeners, whether they paid for the course or not, and for at least a year's duration. Refusal could even jeopardize the "sheepskin" prizes that were recently awarded. It's funny that we were never explicitly told of such eventual shenanigans at the very beginning. Of course, I had paid so did not technically have to comply. After discharging my dental associate, I was back to working six days per week and literally had no time to participate. Additionally, what did that piece of parchment actually do for me? I mean, perhaps it would impress a vole or a weasel, but what about envious human gardeners? I think not. And I later found out from a few volunteering former pupils that most of the questioning phone calls were not easily answered. It was anguishing sitting there while listening to a bored widow drone on about why her rhododendrons were failing and what could be done about it. Remember, this was the early nineties, prior to computers being widespread and before Google could quickly answer most queries. Anyway, I kept my framed diploma and reluctantly displayed it on a shelf right next to my wife's; she ended up taking the same course a few years hence. Hottie Blondie also got read the riot act of "mandatory" volunteering, and unsurprisingly also failed to comply. Good on her. The only suckers in our homestead are the ones we pick off the tomato plants. Was the course ultimately worth it? I think so. Over the years, and on numerous occasions, I have referenced the massive gardening textbook which I had bought for that class. Now I rely solely on readily available online information should I get horticulturally hornswoggled. It's all in a days' work for this grumpy gardener.

11

Weed Killing

Although mundane, it is nevertheless the foundation and backbone of nearly every successful backyard garden. Active maintenance and the eradication of upstart, unwanted "weeds" are par for the course for most amateur horticulturists, unless you lay down special black plastic with holes in it for the plants that are preferred. But what we often consider as weeds are legitimate plants; they don't know they are the burden of gardeners. There is a great deal of profundity regarding what most people consider to be undesirable greens. Knowledgeable Native Americans, Herbalists, Naturopaths, back-to-nature freaks, and unattended toddlers often elevate and eat what many gardeners despise. Dandelions, clover, chickweed, plantain, purslane, and goosefoot are but a few examples of edible "weeds," but are widely considered detestable plants that seek to crowd out the "good" veggies. Thus, the battle for their extermination, or at least tacit management, begins. As already written about, my sister and I were the "work mules" and gardening suckers that did a lot of the boring grunt work. That included periodically picking out rocks, picking off insect pests, picking ripened berries and picking weeds by hand. Although sometimes we were issued gnarly hoes and then had at it. Roundup was introduced in 1974, but we kept things "natural" and did not use it. Of course, Grandpa Pete still accomplished the majority of the labor solo, however, we were always deemed available should help be needed. Anyhow, flash forward about five decades and a person can usually find me somewhere around my own vegetable garden or extensive berry patches during some part of every summer day, rain or shine. And the endless "weed battles" continue.… Even though most of my blueberries are inside sturdy chicken wire and top-netted enclosures, they need to be regularly mowed around with a small lawn mower to keep them free of unwanted and encroaching vegetation, especially during the early spring. Being fairly shallow-rooted, they hate to compete with grasses and other undesirable growths. But today, there is no Grandpa Pete. There are also no elderly sets of parents around. In addition, our adult scientist daughter and her family live far away and our live-in and telecommuting attorney son couldn't give a rat's ass about gardens. Although he is the first one out the fuckin' door to snag and eat ripened purple raspberries and blueberries (only the tart Patriot variety)! That leaves only my wife and I to produce the yearly "fruit and veggie" shows. Yet after all that supposed anguish and PTSD (Post Traumatic Seed Disorder) acquired because of my live-in grandfather's messianic zeal towards gardening, here I was slopping around the dirt with my wife and tenderly tending to our own plantings. And, mostly loving it. Wtf? And how do we keep our tiny garden weed-free? Hoe, hoe, and hoe some more. And usually on a daily basis, especially in the early going, and for sure after every hard, soaking rain. Our rows of beets, beans, Swiss chard, zucchini, yellow squash, eggplants all get the "hoe-down" treatment. However, a little straw (not hay) application around our tomatoes and cucumbers is a time saver. Actually, we have tried to apply straw as a weed deterrent in ALL our rows of veggies. It is highly effective but the clean-up and disposal after harvest can be time consuming and tiresome. Although obviating most of the required hand-weeding once it is laid down, straw tends to fail the "purist gardener" test. It does degrade with time, but does not break down like grass or hay, which can each be tilled under in the spring. Laying down special black plastic as a weed-guard with holes punched in it for preferred plants is another option, one that is used by beautiful, "professional" botanical gardens that people often pay to see and fawn over. That's too much for me. But I have used plastic row-sheeting as a weed barrier. However, slugs and other nocturnal undesirables can easily hide under the plastic strips during the daytime. They keep moist in the dank darkness until their respective dinnertimes at night.

Plus, the pliable strips between the plants need to be anchored to the ground (such as with stones) lest a temperamental tempest blows them off into the woods or onto an adjacent neighbor's yard. All of this takes effort, and lots of rocks. Vinegar, boiling water, and mini flame throwers are bantered about in gardening literature as "natural" controls. I have used all three and found them disappointing. They all work, but not great, and with no lasting effects. It is so tempting to use a spritz of Roundup here and there around edible plants, but I resist. Physical barriers, such as straw, plastic and hand weeding are where we've settled. Anyway, in a small garden such as ours, I find it easier to initially spade the rows regularly and then apply straw as needed. Although sometimes I also foolishly wish Grandpa Pete was still around to do the lion's share of the gardening chores. But then again, maybe not. He would probably end up "supervising" my wife and me, much like he did my sister and me back in the day. I think Hottie Blondie and I are plenty motivated to do our OWN supervision and more than capable of "gettin' 'er done."

12

Aquaculture?

Aquaculture, or the raising of aquatic animals for food, is a part of agronomy. You know, salmon farming, etc. And since I have a man-made pond in my backyard, could I or should I make it a part of watery agriculture and reap the benefits of freshwater seafood? No. Snakes, crayfish, goldfish, salamanders, frogs, turtles, and underwater insects make up the bulk of the natural vertebrates and invertebrates living in that miniscule body of water. It would be a herculean task to convert it into a protein-producing, outdoor, foody wet-market. Of course, in a bona fide lack-of-food emergency, and not in the wintertime, we COULD feast on filet-of-goldfish and Cajun-spiced "mudbug" (crawfish) gumbo! Anyway, the local herons and kingfishers stop and shop in our pond all the time, extracting their fill while I numbly gaze at them from my house. I used to ACTIVELY try to dissuade carnivorous waterfowl from landing, but it was tough work making those majestic birds change their culinary routines. And they always seem to come back for seconds. My daughter was taking a college class in ornithology and during a swampy field trip she suddenly, and involuntarily, started running to chase away a seldom-seen Great Blue Heron much to the horror of the visibly distraught professor and onlooking fellow students. She apologized, but matter-of-factly stated that it was her "job" as a teenager to dispatch any pesky aerial assaults on "her" pond to help save the critters within. Her fellow undergrad students were wide-eyed and speechless and probably thought she was not right in the head. Who thinks beautiful and rarely spotted birds are a pestilence? Well, they obviously didn't know her very well! She loved "her" creepy-crawly pals who inhabited the drink and didn't take kindly to feathery interlopers dispatching them. But she passed the course and graduated with distinction, with a baccalaureate degree in Applied Zoology from the top university in Canada. And after earning a doctorate in Entomology, she was even more protective of her "freshwater friends" whenever she came home for a visit. Old habits die hard, and it was nostalgic to see her gallop outside at a moment's notice, waving her arms about and yelling at the naughty kingfisher just as he was about to take the plunge for a tasty treat. Getting back to the pond, it was originally made because back-fill was needed for our house when it was being built. The more dirt that was required, the deeper and wider the future pond became. The area was low-lying to begin with and the resultant puny dug-out quickly filled up with rainwater. It is ten feet deep at its max in the middle and approximately 50 feet wide by 100 feet long, with a small cadre of cattails lining one oval end and a grass-lined edge around the rest of the periphery. A cleverly laid underground pipe connected to a long roofline house gutter feeds it every time it rains, preventing the water level from falling drastically low. And as stated above, besides artificially stocked with goldfish, it contains most of the naturally occurring plants and animals found in a typically healthy, self-sustaining ecosystem. And though very small it has been periodically, albeit briefly, graced by Canada Geese, various species of ducks, wandering beavers, and muskrats. Even male snapping turtles stop by to breed with the same old, gnarly, submerged female who has lived on the muddy bottom for decades! After mating, she makes a rare appearance every spring while crawling out onto our lawn. She invariably lays her large clutch of eggs near our blueberry bushes. However, the ensuing treks of the emerged hatchlings, who desperately search for the safety of the pond, are undoubtedly harrowing. In addition to many nocturnal animals who need to quaff their thirsts, unruffled White-tailed deer regularly drink from the small body of water as well, although early mornings are their preferred times. We continue to enjoy our pond's silvery and gleaming beauty and have learned to tolerate the many hungry animals, including

crayfish-loving raccoons and water snakes, that seek
to steal a fishy or froggy meal from it, respectively.

13

Staying Strong

Fresh air and out-of-doors work are a refreshing combination that supposedly rejuvenates the body, or so some people say. However, I think it's the other way around. I find that a sound physical countenance is required PRIOR to venturing into the "wild," if only for light backyard gardening and other mild horticultural quests. In other words, you have to be fit before you pick up that pickaxe and start swingin', Tarzan! Nothing sucks more than developing a backache or sore muscles/joints the day after a seemingly innocuous and mindful jaunt among the vegetables or berry bushes. Necessary planting, hoeing, weeding, etc. can be taxing for even the most well-seasoned gardeners. Therefore, my remedy is to be as strong and limber as possible, not only for my sporty endeavors such as daily pickleball playing, but for the physical rigors of yard and veggie management. A few of my previous comedic literary offerings touch upon the absurdities related to my health and fitness pursuits. It has not been smooth sailing for this cussing curmudgeon. As a retired and doddering dullard in the fourth quarter of life, with no time-outs remaining, everything is now a plus, or a minus! During my sixty-five years on this planet,

I've done battle with chronic Lyme disease, have absorbed an exorbitant and unwarranted amount of psychological, job-related stress (my advice is NOT to become an empathetic pharmacist or dentist. Better to be a flimflammer, corrupt politician, slumlord, online con artist, or porn star), *suffered* from marriage, and became an unappreciated male parent. I have also slogged through myriad of acute illnesses, sports injuries, and unsuccessfully tried a multitude of diets, supplements, workouts, cardiovascular conditioning drills, etc., etc. What a loser, right? Nevertheless, and to paraphrase the title of a great song by the rock band Triumph, "I have fought the good fight!" And not only to stay alive, but to remain in SOME kind of shape – yes, round is a shape. Holy hell, it's an ongoing longevity-war and an uphill battle to keep my boyish physique. LMAO. In reality I'm losing it, except for my slowly widening girth, as per the *normative* human experience. Fuck me. However, in hindsight, I have found that restrictive, cult-like and austere eating-lifestyles (such as strict fasting regimens) are not sustainable for the long term and never worked for me. Although, I'm strongly starting to think that the quantity of calories ingested IS causally related to putting on that dreaded poundage. Anyhow, here are a few of my shovel ready health "secrets," if you can call them that. And not that I'm preaching from my supposed healthy-high-horse, or that I stick to all of them on a daily basis because LIFE still happens. In a nutshell, this nut tries to adhere to a calorie restricted, VARIED, Paleo-DASH combo-diet combined with VARIED exercises and sports. In summary, I try to methodically undereat unprocessed, REAL food, and like a shark, I keep moving this same old carcass EVERY SINGLE DAY. "Move it to lose it." However, am I now an allegedly svelte specimen of elderly manhood? Not really. Do I resemble an ancient Greek God, or do I look more like a Goddamn Greek? Lol. Nevertheless, the above-mentioned dietary and sporty habits SEEM to work for me. Do I always follow my own advice? Hell no! However, the trick is to have the wherewithal to quickly get back on your preferred *wagon* whenever you fall off. Borrowing the catchphrase of WWE wrestling icon John Cena, "Never Give Up!" Although, like most Hollywood stars and professional athletes secretly do, perhaps the off-label usage of Ozempic, steroids, or the employment of a personal nutritionist/fitness trainer would indeed work miracles for me and I would finally appear buff, while in the buff. Who knows? Perhaps not. Lastly, according to that insufferable New Age guru and deep thinking *choreboy* Deepak Chopra, inflammation is the underlying culprit of most diseases, mainly chronic ones. And it is likely exacerbated by increased bodily weight. Among his many other philosophical and psychological tenets, he strongly suggests mindful food choices, anti-anxiety/ relaxation therapies and staying in motion to thwart or eliminate inflammation's insidious effects. I wholeheartedly agree. It's basically a commonsense approach to eating and a logical version of an overall wellness plan to feel better. Of course, I am RETIRED now and seem to have ample time for realigning my priorities in life which include being nutritionally balanced and physically active. Not only to keep UP my relative stamina and core strength for sports and horticultural pursuits, but for frequent and consensual coitus with Hottie Blondie - my wife of over four decades. Yeah, baby! Winning! And now for something completely different. Well, not really. All that bending-over, pulling, pushing, and swearing. Who said senior sex and gardening were relaxing and rewarding pastimes? Wowzers! Nevertheless, being skeleto-muscularly prepared for life in general translates well to diminished gardening fatigue and less bodily aches and pains. Of course, no one can stop the aging process, but hopefully being somewhat in shipshape will make horticultural forays less stressful on the body and more enjoyable all around.

14

Brigette's Meadow

Okay, I was a failed apple grower. There, I said it. But what resulted after two decades of fruitless anticipation was something much more satisfying and ecologically sound. Let me explain: With great zeal and determination, I singlehandedly cut and coifed my newly bought three-acre parcel of land. Not only getting it ready for my future home, but preparing it for as much green lawn as possible. That meant brush hogging the acreage on weekends (I was still working full time back then) and "taming" it into some semblance of suburban paradise. After the strenuous work of clearing the unwanted small trees, grasses, weeds and scrub, now it came time for planting. And a mini apple orchard was top of mind and on the list of "fun" things to plant and easily reap the benefits of. I had already plopped blueberry, purple raspberry, and huckleberry bushes into the ground and now it was time to stick six young greenhouse-bought Honeycrisp saplings into the dirt: a half dozen prize plants, which would undoubtedly yield bushels of delicious, mouth-watering, homegrown pomes. Ha, ha. Alas, I tried everything to make them give me fruit. I studied appropriate books and videos. I even consulted apple-growing farmers and gardening specialists to learn how to properly develop adults from young saps. Nothing. It was so frustrating. My dwarf trees were growing, but year after year they produced *bupkis. Nada*, zilch, a big fat zero. But how was this possible? People always said that I had a way with the photosynthetic crowd. So, why was I failing so badly when my property was virtually surrounded by successful commercial apple orchards? If they could grow them, why couldn't I? It was the same sun, soil, and sod. I don't know, but on a few occasions my wife had to verbally restrain me from raiding one of those apple farms to rip out some of their newly planted trees and transplant them on my land. I was that pissed off and desperate. During the summers and fall, I saw plenty of foliage but no apples forming on my darn trees. Obviously, harvest time was always a big 'ole let down. I was told to have patience. However, after twenty-plus years of getting nothing-burgers, all six finally got a well-deserved chop. Fuck them. And what replaced them? Why, a meadow! A meadow? Yes. After all that initial investment of time and sweaty effort to get rid of unwanted growth in that area of my land, now I became excited to witness the formation and maturation of a planned meadow. It is a 50-foot by 50-foot parcel surrounded by immaculately mowed grass and was originally destined to be a haven for all sorts of wildlife, including insects, mammals, and birds. It did not disappoint and continues to this day as a renewable reservoir of "nature" amid my large "manmade" lawn. In honor of my entomologist daughter, I proudly named it Brigette's Meadow, complete with a posted metal sign that says just that. She gets a kick out of seeing it every time she and her family visit. Now a few words about this "back to nature" creation, or should I say, a return to basics. Remember, my whole property was once a huge grassy and woody meadow. Anyhow, there are a few things to consider when purposely growing and managing one. First and foremost, I wanted to have a hospitable habitat for all the meadow-loving animals that I had displaced years prior in my determination to have as much *clean* property as possible, one that looked esthetically manicured and taken care of. A messy and unkempt spot in the middle of this Shangri-La was a mental departure for me, but it was a project I initiated nonetheless. So, after the removal of my failed apple trees, I simply let the grass "grow wild" in that small area. I mowed the surrounding lawn and watched as the many different types of plants and flowers took over the said piece of ground. At this nascent time, I inserted a sturdy metal pole and topped it with a blue bird house. I also introduced some colorful wildflowers to the mix by liberally sprinkling seed packets onto the emerging greenery. In no time there were all kinds of naturally occurring weeds and plants vying for life in that section. After donning some long rubber boots, I routinely and carefully walk through it. Whenever poison ivy, or something prickly or woody rears its ugly head, I methodically cut it down. The place is reserved for a human-friendly meadow and not for a budding mini forest or toxic leafy enclave. And I have succeeded. It has become a welcoming, weed-infested, mini jungle with protruding Black-eyed Susans, tall Timothy, alfalfa, Goldenrod stalks, and clumps of leafy vegetation that I do not readily recognize. But the miniscule fauna seems to love it. Living in it are crickets, as well as grasshoppers, leafhoppers, mantids, butterflies, ambush bugs, bees, wasps, snakes, voles, mice, rabbits, etc. It has quickly become a homey habitat for a panoply of appreciative wildlife to live and breed in. Even recalcitrant and finicky Bluebirds nest yearly in my nest box offering. But this thick thatch has to be properly administered. There is no right or wrong, however, some knowledgeable gardening pundits insist that yearly mowing of a meadow is beneficial. I have never done this. To date, my approach to the meadow mirrors my attitude regarding flatulence: let it rip and let it grow! Anyway, it is recommended that the meadow be cut to 4-6 inches in height every fall and the trimmings either raked up or left as mulch. Most resident animals will not suffer because they are either dead or hibernating.

And most plants are in the same straits. For what it's worth, I guess mowing it down allows it to "start anew" the following year. November is the month I selectively prune my now-dormant blueberry bushes and vertically edge-trim the intentionally made "shrub-fence" that borders most of my property. During the other three seasons, maintaining the meadow is easy, except for the above-mentioned walk-throughs to eradicate truly undesirable and/or noxious plants. I enjoy watching the tiny meadow grow, knowing that even though it may look unruly and out-of-place, it greatly benefits nature's naturally found critters. It continually serves as a source of safety and sustenance for all creatures, great and small.

15

Fencing

American poet Robert Frost coined the phrase "good fences make good neighbors" in his 1914 poem "Mending Wall." That seminal sentence and overused cliché refers to mutual respect and acknowledged personal space between neighboring parties. It also refers to abject physical barriers to help maintain a sense of privacy and ensuing wellness. Private property in America is sacrosanct and frequently the bastion of righteous self-defense and stand-your-ground laws. Having said all that, how does fencing, or barrier placement, relate to gardening? Well, if you don't want disagreeable dolts chewing up your leafy veggie plot, a fence of some sort is probably necessary. And I'm not talking about "bugs and slugs" that might put a few holes in some leaves here and there. I'm speaking of rascally rodents, such as rabbits and woodchucks, that can really sink their respective teeth into growing beans and bok choy, thereby ruining an otherwise good gardening season before it even gets out of the ground. They aren't content to nibble on readily available weeds and grasses. No, the newly growing savory sprouts and luscious leaves are the "cat's meow" for many nocturnal and crepuscular, four-legged creatures. Now, there are obviously

commercial deterrents available to help prevent the
onslaught of animals that are attracted to the juicy
tender vittles of a newly planted garden. However, the
store-bought powders and repellant pellets that can be
sprinkled in and around the garden's edges are a joke.
Even natural substances like cayenne pepper, oils,
moth balls, and mustard do not work well. Insects
can be kept at bay with poisonous products such as
Rotenone and Sevin (which I personally do not use),
but hungry and loathsome mammalian beasts are not
easily deterred by most foul-tasting or odorous agents.
Therefore, I have found that killing, humanely
trapping and prevention are some of the obvious ways
for keeping warm-blooded critters and their
respective snouts out of the vegetables. Shooting
varmints, where permissible, can be fundamentally
satisfying, but "there is always more where they came
from," as the saying goes. Trapping with Hav-A-Hart
traps is an option that I have used many times,
especially for unwanted chipmunks that make
burrows in and around my house. These underground
tunnels are often abandoned and can become prime
real estate for swarming and stinging Yellowjackets
come fall. Anyway, when using humane traps,
woodchucks, rabbits, and deer (too big, duh!) are
savvy and cannot easily be enticed or fooled with
veggie bait. That's where fencing comes in. A stout
physical barrier, such as made with three-foot-tall

chicken wire, is the best way to keep out starving, furry vegans. But it takes some work to erect the permanent, or removable, staked structures. And the resulting metal-wood contraptions encompassing the various plots of desired growth can be less than esthetic-looking to the discerning eye. Too damn bad. Even though I can be a fussy, nitpicking neatnik, when it comes to self-produced produce, I don't care how unsightly the fencing appears. Large farms can get away with a certain percentage of vegetable loss whereas I wish to pick every last stinkin' beet and bean in my miniscule "Garden of Eden." I can't afford to give away lunches to freeloading furballs. In other words, I selfishly want ALL my well-deserved fruits and veggies for me and my family, only. Am I wrong for thinking like a *dumb* animal? Don't answer that!

16

Digging in the Dirt

Unlike Digger the Badger, an infamous anthropomorphic animal character in Thornton Burgess's series of *Old Mother West Wind* children's stories, the titular word Digging is used partly in jest. And partly not. Gardening and most horticultural pursuits involve some kind of spading of the Earth's thin crust, and the words plowing, hoeing, mulching, shoveling, raking, etc. usually denote humans getting at least partially dirty. Anyway, besides the alleged mental and physical therapeutic benefits of working with plants, is there also something profoundly soothing and possibly mystical that occurs when physically being so near the soil? Especially when immersed in it with naked hands and feet? In Reiki, there is a technique called Grounding, whereby the "healer" usually positions herself at the foot of the treatment table and lightly grasps the feet of the "patient." And, while firmly standing, she manifests the intention of being solidly planted. This is done to physically *ground* the patient's body to the Earth's "energy" field. It fosters a feeling of calmness, connectedness, and seeks to focus and rebalance wayward "energies." But should most of today's modern post-agrarian-era humans willfully regress and shuck off shoes, socks, and gloves to become purposely filthy in a New-Age Reiki-type-of-way when gardening? I don't know, but my wife handles seeds and seedlings barehanded and covers up the plantings barefooted. As an advanced Reiki teacher, she claims it greatly benefits her to be so intimately in touch with the raw elements. Okay, then…. I wear industrial strength Merrell "work shoes," and fight weeds and handle gardening implements with leather gloves on. Although also an advanced Reiki practitioner, perhaps it's the retired dentist in me that still wants to "save" my dexterous hands from any deleterious stains, rashes, abrasions, cuts, and bruises. But that's just me. Speaking of topsoil, let's examine a few things. There are many soil types with varying levels of "nutrient based fertility" that influence what can and can't be successfully grown. Let me elucidate from memory. All that "earthy" knowledge I haphazardly learned from Mr. Gloflop in ninth grade (1973-74) Regents-level Earth Science is coming back to me now. No, not really. It was a bitch, with a new hippie teacher, a new hip textbook and a brand-new syllabus. Maybe the words "silly bus" would be more apropos as to the way Mr. Gloflop drove that class. If it wasn't for desperately studying the info in The Barron's Earth Science Regents review book, the entire class would have ostensibly failed the difficult Regents exam at the end of the scholastic year. I lucked out with a 91 on that test, and then promptly forgot most of the nightmarish course and its dubious teachings. But to be fair, most people agree that high school Earth Science is a tough row to hoe. Anyhow, back to *Joe Dirt*, so to speak: approximately 500 million years in the past, during the Paleozoic Era and late Cambrian Period (the time of the trilobites), the northeast United States was covered with a shallow ocean. Then, 400 million years later the climate changed – obviously caused by the farts and belches of "non-woke" dinosaurs – making our part of the country high and dry. And then, much, much later, the Ice Age hit. When the huge, North American-covering, Wisconsin glacier finally retreated approximately eleven thousand years ago - obviously due to global warming caused by all the prehistoric, "non-woke," knuckle-dragging cavemen - the resultant and newly remaining soil was basically of four types: sand, silt, clay, and loam. Of course, there were boulders mixed in, especially at the edges of the melted ice, such as the huge rocks still found near Long Island Sound and the Connecticut coast. The dirt in the Catskills where I grew up was very rocky, amethyst-colored and easily became mud during rainy conditions. It was highly fertile, however. My new home soil in the Capital region is a sandy-loam variety with a composition of 60% sand, 10% clay, and 30% silt. Though vastly different from my childhood turf, it is also considered well-draining and good for veggie agriculture, including amateur gardening. Nevertheless, because my particular property harbors underground deposits of calcium, iron, and sulfur, the tapped well water needs to be conditioned with a sophisticated water softening system. Furthermore, some underground-grown vegetables, such as carrots, potatoes, turnips, and parsnips, end up tasting poorly because of the foul and odorous minerals imbedded in the original topsoil. Now, over the years I have added layers of organic, clean, store-bought soil to supplement my garden and perk up the existing terra firma. You would think that there would be some improvement due to the additions of unadulterated sod, but no. Somehow, the carrots still tasted like crap, and I stopped growing them as a result. However, the beets are okay, and the surface-grown plants are unaffected. Does that motivate me to play mad scientist or chemist (a few ounces of Miracle-Gro here and there during the growing season does not count) with my garden every spring? Not really. I add topsoil as needed to compensate for erosion and attrition, rototill every late May just before planting, and then get at it with my wife – the planning and planting, as well.

17

Woodchuck Woes

Some human connoisseurs call them land beavers, whistle pigs or groundhogs, names which sound innocuous and even noble. In my boyhood locale we dismissively referred to them as woodchucks, a word presumably derived from the original Algonquin Indian term: "wuchaks." These stubborn, subterranean rodents are a curse to cattle farmers and amateur gardeners, alike. Their holey homes can break an unsuspecting cow's leg if stepped into. Likewise, even suburbs are not spared woodchucks' tenacity and tendency to readily set up housekeeping. Though wary of people, they are also brave enough to emerge from their unnatural homes - underneath sheds and man-made structures - to wreak havoc on surrounding plants and unprotected vegetables. Appearing roly-poly and placid, these animals are vegetarian eating machines with fecund females able to produce young in seemingly unfavorable locations. Wild woodchucks are not the same as the anthropomorphic character Johnny Chuck in the *Old Mother West Wind* series of children's books by Thornton Burgess (my kids grew up listening to and reading these wonderful volumes). While Johnny Chuck is portrayed as lazy, slow-witted, and good-natured, the same cannot be said for a real-life groundhog. They can be very mean-spirited, are quick to bite, and often excrete a malodorous musk when threatened at close range. They are cautious and quickly hide if even the least bit of perceived danger spooks them. Of course, the more they get used to human traffic, the bolder they become. They can even be domesticated (i.e. "weather forecaster" Punxsatawney Phil comes to mind every Groundhog Day). My old man used to sight his expensive, Finnish-made, Sako-brand rifle on them just before deer hunting season began. It was a father and son autumnal ritual at our house. And let me tell you, it sometimes took hours quietly lying in tall grass on farmer's fields, approximately fifty yards away, while waiting for one to pop up out of its burrow before Pop popped it with a 30-06 slug. And the "good times" continued when the old man would go into my bedroom, quietly open a window, aim his costly 22-caliber, scoped, HIGH STANDARD-brand target pistol and "plug a chuck" in the backyard, one that was obviously getting too close to the garden! But those shootin' days are long gone. Hav-A-Hart traps are what I use to sometimes trap and relocate these furry pests from around my own garden. And when trapped, using parsley as bait, they are not docile creatures at all. As mentioned, they can become very aggressive and do not like to be involuntarily confined, nor poked and prodded by humans. And lastly, they need to be released at least 500 yards away to prevent a reappearance. Although considered a very good marksman with most deadly weapons, I have found that barriers work best against any springtime woodchuck onslaught. My three sheds and gazebo are set above the dirt, but are purposely packed with bricks, large stones, and debris around the surrounding, ground-level periphery. And enterprising woodchucks STILL periodically manage to find a rocky crevice or seam to squeeze through to set up a home. *Oi Vey*, what a headache! And sometimes I will securely block up the entrance hole only to have them re-dig it out, over and over again. It can be a test of wills to ferret out these *nudges* and to have them vacate my yard. But why am I on such a seemingly mean mission to eradicate these animals if my garden is barricaded and impenetrable? Please, allow me: years ago, before I wised up, I ended a growing season sans beans, lettuce, squash, and zucchini because I was too late in putting up fencing after the veggies started to sprout. That was infuriating enough, but then I noticed that my sheds and gazebo were diagonally sagging, and subsequently their doors would not shut properly. Holy Leaning Tower of Pisa, Batman! That's right, Robin. Not the Penguin, Riddler or Joker, but Woodchucks!!! If the woodchuck entrance holes are at the corners of small structures, it causes the soil to collapse in those areas and the buildings to tilt. Now I had to jack up the sheds and gazebo and rebase the ground with stones before lowering the buildings back into their respective and level positions. It was a lot of hard work, darn it. Well, through meticulous stonework, surveillance, and trapping, I finally put a kibosh on that dominant paradigm. However, once in a while I will get a furry fool that's unknowingly hell-bent on making my life miserable, one that cavalierly seeks to mow down my veggies AND establish a domicile on my property. No can do. I pity the rookie rodent who wants to play games with a humanoid senior citizen. It can be hard to outsmart an experienced old duffer! Of course, my suburban-dwelling, Connecticut-based daughter has a similar and continuing woodchuck problem in her back yard, as well. She and her husband have even gone so far as to bury the reinforced garden fence a foot underground as part of the permanent barricade that encompasses the vegetable-growing area, which is mere yards from their back porch. But alas, try as they might, they cannot keep those whistle pigs out from underneath their large shed. It has almost become a joke. The mother woodchuck and her brood can often be seen emerging, cavorting, and feeding right next to the forbidden veggie plot. Oh, they badly want to get in, but cannot. However, there seems to be a tenuous truce established between my daughter's family and the resident groundhog family. It has gone so far that my baby granddaughter owns an authentic-looking, stuffed toy woodchuck. Oh, boy, say it ain't so. However, I'm the foolish and "senile" grandpa who bought it for her. Lol.

18

Of Mice and Sheds

For this next tale, my addled brain decided to use a paraphrased version of the title of John Steinbeck's famous literary classic. Although the second half of the titular sentence could have just as easily included the words: homes, attics, automobiles, machinery, and even abandoned birdhouses. However, we shall stick to field mice and sheds. We won't discuss the importance of the white, albino variety found in biologic testing laboratories around the world. Or those that are sold in pet stores, either as food for pets or as pets themselves. Most humans who choose to live in bucolic, country settings usually deal with prolific and pugnacious mice. Even city dwellers often put up with a similar but different species of *MOUSE*. What is it about these tailed vermin that place them near the top of most lists as despicable, pesky pests? Wait a minute. Far away from urban settings it is PEOPLE that have encroached upon mice and THEIR living spaces, not the other way around. Nevertheless, these tiny animals have the *chutzpah* to opportunistically inhabit any and all "vacant" structures in their wide-ranging territories. Colonizing stationary outdoor objects are a no-brainer; most of these miniscule mammals think it's for them! Thanks a lot, you stupid humans. But they have been unwanted and most unwelcome animals since ancient times infesting food depots, granaries, and primitive homes. It seems that mankind is a welcome wagon for mice to glom onto, especially during their times of starvation and loss of habitat. In fact, mouse populations tend to grow wherever there are Homo sapien suckers who unwittingly provide them with shelter and sustenance. Anyway, I have three sheds and three times the problems trying to keep these critters at bay. And although mice have never hurt my garden per se, they continually invade my home and sully up my sheds. The ubiquitous field mouse is usually six to seven inches in length with a grey-brown furry exterior, a white belly, and a long hairy tail. They mostly inhabit fields and meadows. They also like to live near a steady food supply. And as omnivores, they can live nearly everywhere. However, when it comes to raising a mouse family, or to hunkering down during wintertime, an enclosed structure with easy access is where they choose to go. Hence, my shed and house situations. A house mouse is a different species than their field compatriots and the two do not interbreed. The house mice are usually smaller, with mostly grey fur and small, hairless tails. Not to digress, but in 1986 when my young wife and I were living in a flea-bitten, cockroach-infested, barely one-bedroom, walk-up apartment over a shitty Chinese restaurant in lower Manhattan, a mother house mouse and her four babies would ritually exit our kitchen stove on selected evenings and join us in the living area. All of us, the unperturbed and seated rodents included, would be glued to the TV watching the New York Mets baseball team have a magical fall, ending in a World Series championship. Well, at least it SEEMED as though the "tame" mice were watching…. Anyhow, field and house mice both have a tendency to store food, which can become a major source of unwanted contamination and persistent odor. And speaking of smells, the nest of a field mouse is usually packed with putrefying foodstuffs, filled with oval-shaped droppings, and stinks of urine. It is not a pleasant encounter. The nests, which are handmade inside of lawn tractor engines, underneath rototillers, in a distant corner under a piece of tarp, etc., have layers of gathered yarn, leaves, ripped-up cloth, and whatever the mother mouse locally gathers and feels is comfy for her inevitable forthcoming litter of pups. But just what makes the small, field mouse species so darn detestable, yet fascinating? Seeing as how they usually live for up to six months in the wild and are preyed upon by a posse of larger animals and birds, field mice have had to adapt and use their pea brains to the utmost level to stay alive. Firstly, they reach sexual maturity after three weeks of life. And despite their short lifespans, they can produce up to 17 batches of offspring in a year, with 4-7 baby mice born per birth. Populations of mice stay high even though the death rate is commensurate. Other factors influencing their seeming omnipresence include living in colonies, diets, and a mostly hidden, nocturnal lifestyle. However, what makes them such diabolical diablos are their tendencies to eat "everything in sight" AND cause collateral damage. They chew on electrical wires, can ruin automobile and farm-machinery engines, and burrow into house insulation and through walls causing loss of heat, etc. Not to mention they can be natural reservoirs of the Lyme spirochete as well as other viral and bacterial diseases, ones that can potentially infect humans. A mouse infestation in a shed is mainly a nuisance; a mouse infestation of a home can be serious and even deadly. Ok, Tom was always unsuccessful at catching his clever cartoon nemesis named Jerry. And he was a cat! So how do we mere mortals stop these little rascals from multiplying, invading, multiplying, eating, multiplying…? You get the point. It can be a real challenge. The obvious weapons at our disposal for instant eradication are traps and poisons. Yes, they work. However, cleaning up the home and shed interiors of mouse-inviting trash is a good way to start. Humanely using exclusionary barrier techniques and so-called mice-repelling oils and scents, such as balsam products and dryer sheets, can be other routes to follow. Lastly, contracting a professional pest control company to seal up a home and go the "whole nine yards" can be efficacious, albeit expensive. Remember, mice can get through the tiniest cracks in search of food and warmth making them a formidable opponent, especially during the winter season. In conclusion, I have seen field mice and their nests in empty birdhouses that I neglected to take down in time, in every nook and cranny in my admittedly porous sheds, and inside idle engines that eventually need to be cleaned and repaired. And this onslaught keeps happening right under my watchful eye, so to speak. So, what do I do? I look out for mouse droppings in my home and out-buildings, I have traps in my attics, and place highly scented dryer sheets and Cab botanical rodent repellent sacks (balsam fir extract) underneath my lawn tractors starting in the fall. And that's about it. I do the best that I can and still get bushwhacked by these cunning furballs. My current cats are indoor-only (too many coyotes and fisher-cats around). We once had long-lived, indoor/outdoor kitties (Sherman and Skyler) that were keen hunters. But they did not make much of a difference; you know how cats are. I couldn't exactly instill upon them the concept of religiously guarding the sheds and house night after night to keep rodents away. Oh, well. While my present felines (Dexter the Cat and Josie Jo) hear the occasional scratching of a momma mouse in our bedroom walls, they can effectively do nothing about it. Once in a while, a mouse will die in between those very walls and the affected room will reek for days before the unpleasant odor slowly dissipates. Ah, fresh air and frontier living. My wife and I signed up for it, brought up our children here, and unfortunately continue to unintentionally raise multitudes of mice, as well.

19

Backyard Scoundrels

To be fair, most corralled and humanized suburban backyards are carved out of habitats that formerly housed a plethora of naturally occurring wildlife. My home and surrounding "tamed" acreage are no exceptions. Technically speaking, our resultant landscaped three-acre parcel is more than a typical building lot; it has natural wood barriers on three sides and abuts a forever wild side at the very back. It's like living in the boondocks, with neighbor houses barely visible through the thick and shrubby property lines. Add to this mix a manmade pond, and the formerly overgrown, marshy farm field once again hosts a bevy of untamed wild critters who decided that living with people isn't all that bad. And my family and I are smack dab in the middle of it! Although it is less of a nightmare than expected. After all, my wife had many physical run-ins with ill-tempered moose, bats, waterfowl, porcupines, muskrats, wolves, bobcats, beavers, coyotes, foxes and Black bears during her formative years in the Adirondacks. My Catskills upbringing had me face less formidable adversaries such as deer, groundhogs, rabbits, snakes, spiders, squirrels, and mice. I guess she has quite a few up on me…. Anyway, suffice it to say that in the beginning we were both adequately prepared, at least psychologically, to handle any ornithological, reptilian, amphibious, or furry foes that stupidly wanted to cross paths with us. However, some of the truly vile creatures that continually make our land their own included unwanted mosquitos, deer flies, black flies, wasps, and ticks. They are miniature representatives of the animal kingdom, and all can bring much wretchedness to outdoor-loving people. Mosquitos bite and suck, deer and black flies bite really hard and really suck, wasps are often merciless, stinging marauders, and ticks can be disease-carrying no-goodniks. Now, most acquaintances remark that I SEEM to like most animals. That may be true, however as a vegetable gardener and berry grower, that longstanding love affair often fades rather quickly when dealing with veggie and fruit-plucking pariahs. Most of nature's meaty lifeforms, including humans, tend to be opportunistic in nature. Yet here I am setting the backyard table with "free" victuals for *animules* to eat at and complaining when they do. And then I have the temerity to further tease these same creatures by fencing them out. Of course, most are unknowing nuisances, yet some try hard to aggravate me at every turn. Let's start with the hair-covered beasts first, and in no particular order of orneriness. As talked about in previous vignettes, woodchucks, rabbits, and mice make up the bulk of the mammalian troublemakers seeking to get happy meals and rent-free living quarters from unprotected structures, gardens, and berry patches. But what about those innocent-looking, yet devilish chipmunks? You know, the twitchy striped squirrels with their erect tails that seem to have boundless energy. The ones that make unsightly burrows next to homes, sheds and in the yard; underground lairs that frequently become occupied with nasty Yellowjackets come fall. Yes, those chipmunks! Well, they may look cute, but are in fact formidable and undeterred rodents which are often difficult to eradicate from around human habitation. Hundreds of distant releases later after using small Hav-A-hart traps, flooding the holes with cayenne pepper-infused water and/or Clorox, and filling up the dens with dirt have done little to curtail these ground squirrels from nesting where they please. But I always put up a good fight and occasionally win. Yay! Next up are coyotes. Some "knowledgeable" folks say that coydogs are the local mischievous minions, but others insist that honest to goodness coyotes are the actual wild and predatory canids found in our area. Who knows, perhaps both are here? We have heard them howling from time to time, and I was rudely surprised by one nonchalantly running across our lawn in the daytime. Luckily it most likely did not have rabies because it possibly could have attacked me. These large predators, coydog or coyote, are hunters, omnivorous scavengers, and can be all-around headaches for farmers and suburban dwellers alike. They mainly have carnivorous appetites and will eat most animals that can be easily killed, including domestic dogs and cats. I blame "them" for dispatching our beloved indoor/outdoor cats Felicia and Mr. Peabody in succession, many years ago. Although our original cat siblings, Sherman and Skyler, lived mainly out-of-doors for close to twenty years apiece, they somehow managed to stay alive. Either they were smart, lucky, or had used up their respective nine lives when they finally passed. Our present felines Dexter the Cat and Josie Jo are indoor-only, and we will keep it that way for ALL our future cats. Raccoons, those dastardly denizens of the dark, are not really a people problem unless unprotected organic garbage is left outside. However, if you are a hungry "mudbug" looking to pick off grass at night near the edges of our pond, then you may become dinner for these voracious masked mammals. Over the years, I have seen hundreds of raccoon footprints on the muddy shoreline of the pond as evidence of their nocturnal foraging for delectable crayfish. The unwary crawdads are ambushed, probably washed anew as per raccoon instincts, and then crunched up and swallowed. C'est la vie; that's life in the fast lane of nature. Beavers!

What can I say? Yes, we've had them too. Well, at least one that I spotted on a summer day leisurely using our dinky pond as a personal bathtub. But why was it there, with multiple and much larger surrounding bodies of water? I don't know, but it was a bitch trying to get that buck-toothed and hirsute dam-maker out of the damn drink. I yelled from shore, and it merely slapped its broad tail quite loudly against the surface as if to flip me off. Great, just great. But I had to get it out of there because the pond banks are home to many aspen trees which beavers are fond of cutting down. I went back into the house and returned with my trusty, pump-action, pellet rifle. Some people say that I am a very good shot (though born in western New York State, I grew up in Delaware County and have handled various loaded guns from a tender age) and the beaver soon found that out. However, no matter how many times I hit home, the mangy mammal merely shrugged off the ineffectual .177 caliber rounds and kept right on swimming in the sunshine. I stopped shootin' when I realized that none of the bullets were penetrating that thick, matted fur. However, I refused to leave the area and the beaver finally got the hint: though imposing, that big hairball with a paddle-like tail was persona non grata. It extricated itself from the water, crossed the cattail threshold adjacent to the lawn, and slowly ambled past the evergreen border at the back of my wooded property. Whew, I had saved my young aspen trees near the pond from those yellowed beaver teeth! Muskrats are often confused with beavers. Nevertheless, they are completely different animals, with different characteristics and temperaments. It was raining one spring afternoon as I was picking up wind-downed sticks and small branches from a small, wooded area next to my pond when I spotted something swimming straight at me. I didn't know what it could be. It was too small to be a beaver and did not look the least bit distressed being in the water. Whatever it was, I gathered that it did not like me, so I decided to run around the pond to the other side. Kind of like playing chicken. Well, that only enraged the shaggy animal, whom I now identified as the semi-aquatic muskrat; the rat-like tail gave it away. I finally relented and walked up to the house, all the while peering over my shoulder to make sure it was in the pond and still in view. I don't like backbiters! However, shortly thereafter, it disappeared. Perhaps running into me dissuaded it from making a burrow in one of the banks to have its young. Or maybe something ate it. I do not know, but it vanished. I recalled that some of my *good old boy* male friends in high school trapped muskrats in shallow streams on their respective farms, skinned them, and then sold the "river mink" pelts. I guess there was a market for that kind of fur, even back in the '70s. And now a few

words about foxes. Clever, cunning, and courageous
are choice words that describe this sleek and beautiful
member of the canine family. Rightfully maligned by
chicken farmers, their omnivorous diets can make
them real pests in suburban settings, as well.
Although mostly dining on birds, frogs, carrion and
small mammals, such as voles and rabbits, foxes can
and will opportunistically nab a small cat, kitten or
tiny dog. Decades ago, my middle shed was finally
cleared of woodchucks trying to establish homes
underneath it. But then a female fox decided that she
wanted to raise her litter of cubs under its wooden
flooring. I had walled up the sides adjacent to the
ground with large rocks after the woodchuck fiasco,
but she found a weak joint in my stony fortification,
dug an entrance tunnel, and set up her nursery. I
noticed her coming and going and shook my head in
laughter. This was going to be easy. I patiently waited
until she left the den and placed a small boulder to
block the hole. Ha, the joke was on me. She dug
around it, displaced other rocks that were in the way,
and was in business once again. Well, this went on for
a few days and I was getting nowhere. Of course, I
consulted the internet and tried ingenious ways of
ridding our property of that fox. She was no physical
threat to me and my family, however, we had outdoor
cats and did hear that foxes can get rabies. Plus, I felt
put-upon. How dare a stupid animal try to get away

with such audacious hubris while on my watch? Urine-soaked socks stuffed into the burrow were summarily cast out. Flexible wire inserted to "stir the pot" accomplished *nada*. Water and stinky liquids poured into the lair were tolerated. Stomping around inside the shed at different times of the day and night did nothing but elicit a few menacing growls. Firecrackers thrown inside the hole exploded and fumed up the entryway, however, the fox did not move away. Gratefully there were no humans around to witness the ongoing shenanigans because I probably resembled a frustrated Elmer Fudd at the end. And there was an end. One fine day in early summer I was startled to see the mother fox and her progeny standing next to the shed and eyeballing me as I stared back. I'm sure they had come out many times before, only I wasn't there to see them. Although my wife did say that she had sometimes seen flashes of orange in the general vicinity of the sheds. Anyway, after that last furry presentation to yours truly, the fox family vanished from their home and my yard. I'm sure they hung around as newbie predators but never again did a bushy-tailed, foxy female use one of my three sheds as a convenient cover for an underground domicile. Bats, bats, and more little brown bats. Though not scoundrels per se, they nonetheless indiscriminately prey upon a large variety of flying insects, including the "good" ones.

My hardy wife had more than a few altercations with them as a teenager, mostly at dusk, and while swimming nude in chilly Adirondack lakes. She did not appreciate batty bats divebombing and buzzing her blonde pate as she swam. Of course, even as a young lady she knew that they were merely after bugs. However, she was always greatly unnerved just the same! Presently, during warm summer evenings when we sometimes take a sit-down break on the back porch to appreciate our yard, it becomes a pleasure observing the bats flit about in the waning shards of sunlight. And a note to those inclined to set up bat houses as a commonsense approach to mosquito control: I had four such professionally made wooden houses which I nailed to trees around my property. They were "guaranteed" to lure bats to roost in them. Then the flying mammals would presumably multiply and keep the renegade insect populations in check. The advertising gimmicks made the endeavor look so natural, organic, and effortless. Unfortunately, no one told the bats that they needed to cooperate. Duh! The bats on my property had homes in the cupola of my gazebo and in nearby abandoned woodpecker holes found in rotted deciduous trees. The bat houses were filled-up with wasps instead. By the way, I took them all down years ago. What a waste. Speaking of a common animal that frequently gets wasted by furry predators, how about some words on rabbits? Okay, here we go: Nice, fluffy, and seemingly gentle creatures, the Eastern Cottontail can be a destructive and persistent *putz* in the garden and berry patch. Fencing and other barrier methods often need to be employed and monitored to deter these determined jumping rodents. Once they acquire a taste for a certain plant, watch out - without physical protection, it will frequently be nibbled to a nub. And with all the fresh grass and clover available in my backyard, you would think that the multitude of roaming bun-buns would be satiated with the plentiful food underfoot, so to speak. But no. These doggone, long-eared galoots (thank you for the expressive lingo, Yosemite Sam) can be a gardener's nightmare. Fortunately, Peter Rabbit and his notoriously extensive kin have mortal enemies. This helps keep their populace from really exploding. Coyotes, dogs, eagles, hawks, fisher cats, foxes, domestic cats (our old cat Sherman used to bring freshly killed rabbits inside the house by dragging it through our cellar-window cat flap – what a mess!) and even large owls snap them up when given the chance. However, rabbits are part of our landscape and even nest in Hottie Blondie's herb garden, underneath the overhanging thyme bush. How can you truly hate these cute and fuzzy bunnies hopping around the yard? Nevertheless, my largely benevolent sentiments shifted many years ago when I found some newly planted and unfenced blueberry plants cut down to smithereens, effectively stunting their growth for years to come. Bad bunnies! Of course, White-tailed deer could have done the damage as well. I wasn't there as an eyewitness when the floral carnage transpired. Like silent shadows, deer are often picturesque moving parts in the suburban background. Wow, what elegant and haughty beauties they tend to be. What statuesque animals they are…. What the hell? Those tick-infested fuckers are mowing down my exposed hostas, arborvitae bushes, and azaleas! Where are all the deer hunters when you need them? Just joshing; well, at least partly. By now most readers are probably questioning my alleged love of "innocent" wildlife. Should my actual credo be that animals are fine, but not in my backyard? Is that it? Am I a duplicitous and senile senior who easily gets irritated at having his rhubarb rubbed the wrong way by "nature"? Most definitely, because this sexagenarian still gets skunked by the bawdy and bold behavior of various four, six, and eight-legged interlopers. And skunks are right up there in the annoyance department. What the heck are they doing to make large swaths of the lawn look like it had an overnight case of pockmarked measles? Why, these striped mammalian *menschen* are merely digging out shallow holes in search of beetle grubs. They are in fact doing landscape architects a favor by decreasing the Japanese beetle populations, but at a cost to the cosmetics of the grass. However, one time my anger boiled over and I baited a large Hav-A-Hart trap with wet cat food and set it in the middle of my yard. And I caught a skunk! Yippee, or not. Trying valiantly to escape, it proceeded to claw furiously at the bottom of the cage and was fast ruining a rectangular section of lawn. Of course, I quickly called our local Animal Control officer to help me out. Meanwhile the beady-eyed and black and white malingerer kept right on scratching through the metal bars until my wife had seen enough. She hurriedly put a blanket over the steel enclosure and deftly lifted the side door to spring the poor prisoner, without the scared scalawag discharging even a small fart – the skunk, that is. By the time Animal Control showed up the next day, the skunky ordeal was long over. However, now I had to work extra hard in order to make the denuded turf look right. Swallowing my wounded pride, I had no choice but to let these nighttime sleuths eat beetle grubs and adult beetles to their hearts' content. No more skunk trapping for me. A little massaging of the small grassy clumps back into place (kind of like divot replacement on the links) is what I continually do to clean up the ongoing yet sporadic nocturnal messes. We have made peace, sort of. Opossums, which will be mentioned again later, are stealthy, peach-stealing thieves that seem to appear out of nowhere at night.

They are omnivorous and DO eat loads of noxious arthropods such as ticks. However, these American marsupials prefer to gobble up hanging fruits, especially those in the nectarine family. Unkempt-looking possums are yet another species of animal with whom I have a tenuous relationship. Last-up on the list of "misbehaving" mammals are moles and voles. Most horticulture enthusiasts, and folks with any size yard, have at the very least seen the telltale markings of these two elusive and velvety critters. In the spring, subterranean moles have a penchant to push up pyramid-shaped piles of dirt along their twisty underground routes. Sometimes huge sections of my property resemble a comical-looking mini volcano field. And the raised-up and long tunnels are disheartening to step on, as well. I realize moles are not after my veggies and instead hunt for worms, grubs and bugs. But my resultant unsightly lawn bugs me, too. Over the years I have tried various means to effectively chase away these ground-dwelling lowlifes. Have I been successful? No. Traps, pouring nasty liquids into their entry holes, inserting vibrating electric spikes into the horizontal passageways, and physically flattening the subterranean burrows have never really worked for me. Some years are worse than others and I cannot predict them with any sense of scientific certainty. However, by summer, the black furry critters and their annoying living quarters seem to fade from view. Actually, moles themselves are rarely seen at any time of year. They are basically banal animals that scarf up dirt-dwelling worms and insects, and aerate the earth at the same time. Without making a mountain out of a molehill, I begrudgingly fold their excavated soil clumps back into the turf before mowing the grass with a Bad Boy, Zero-turn lawn tractor. I have a truce with them; we manage to co-exist. Voles are a slightly different matter. Also called meadow mice and field mice, these tiny, stubby-tailed, straight-line running rodents can be relatively benign or seemingly belligerent. One can often see them scurrying across a street while driving at night. They don't hop, skip, or jump, but often make a straight beeline from one side of the road to the other. Their little legs manage to propel them quite efficiently. But all is not copacetic in my relationship with them. Firstly, they make ungodly, semi-lunar, serpentine surface furrows ending in shallow underground burrows, thoroughfares that ruin the ambience of parts of the lawn. And secondly, voles love to munch on beets and other underground veggies. Trying to eradicate them from around the garden can be problematic. They are frequently determined little tykes and I don't have outdoor cats anymore to squelch their numbers. So, I must defend my plants as best as I can because they easily slip through chicken wire and are great diggers. But truth be told, I have not actively sought to trap them or spread mammal-deterrent pellets near the affected veggies. It's really a "luck-of-the-draw" thing - during every garden growing season. Sometimes they are found in large numbers, other years, not so much. As far as the lawn goes, I routinely tamp the scratched-out sod pieces into place and patch things up after scolding those darn voles out loud. Maybe that helps? I don't know because they always return and probably thumb their little noses at me in disdain.

But now, let's switch gears and discuss the *fiends* who think my yard is their watery oasis; winged and billed creatures that can really put a crimp in happy human habitation: kingfishers, geese, and herons. In addition to the fine feathered friends who swipe my unprotected berries, these three types of fowl always put me in a foul mood whenever they trespass on my peaceful piece of earthly paradise. It's quite alright if they fly overhead and keep on truckin'. However, what greatly vexes me is when these wingnuts decide to land right under my nose. Whenever I see and hear them, my temperature and temper start to rise. The squawky kingfishers always announce their presence within the vicinity of my pond with a series of shrill shrieks. Usually, the presence of a human nearby will make them shy away from landing on an overhanging tree branch or to circle over the water. However, the evidence of their presence is acutely felt whenever I discover dismembered goldfish and crayfish around the property. Sure, other animals eat the same grub, but I have witnessed the Belted Kingfishers dive and fish from a distance; they are highly skilled underwater hunters. Boy, would I like to haul off and belt one, at times! I have yet to find an effective means for keeping the fish and crawdads safe from these determined and cunning birds. Great Blue Herons and their immediate kin, such as the Green Heron and Bittern, wade, stalk, and strike. Be it frogs, fish, crayfish, salamanders, or snakes, these large, dinosaur-derived, flying fowl are persistent, returning time and again for the free buffet. Family members, past and present, have futilely chased these long-beaked and long-necked marauders, but to no avail. When threatened, they simply fly away. Obviously, a zealous and protective koi aquaculturist would probably kill these particular birds of prey. However, I don't foster koi fish and after all, many elitist non-gardeners insist that ALL animals are basically good. %!&&@!! Anyway, Canada Geese take the cake for sheer boldness and perseverance. Though majestic, they are eating and pooping machines. The acidic droppings destroy the grassy lawn and often make the areas next to the pond unwalkable whenever the geese arrive en masse. And that's exactly what I try to prevent from happening every spring. But it's a tall order. I don't mind an infrequent stopover or pitstop by a mated pair; to sit, soak and then slurp a few underwater plants. It's when twenty or more descend from the heavens and refuse to leave that makes me hot and bothered (not just in the bedroom). A large gaggle of uninvited geese can really honk me off. Because once landed, they are difficult to shoo away. Clapping and rock throwing in their general directions often make them move away and duck into the protection of the water. They don't always get the hint to skedaddle. A blustery show of force by an angry human sometimes works, but not always. Oftentimes, and after an ungodly amount of time has elapsed, I simply retreat with the remaining geese still firmly ensconced in the pond. But in my mind, I am thinking of that quote from the fictional Canadian McKenzie brothers of *Great White North* fame: "Take off ya hosers. Take off, eh?" By the way, and frequently touted as a guaranteed preventative, placing phony plastic swans in the pond does NOT work as a disincentive. And constantly repositioning fake coyote decoys around the embankments only serves to frighten my unsuspecting wife. When they do finally depart, the geese invariably leave behind dark green/white, foul-smelling droppings. After the turds harden, I dutifully scrape the remnants off the "burned" grass sections and dispose of the stinky crap. You would think I maniacally hate these birds. Well, yes and no. When a pair and their goslings emerge from the wooded areas by early summer to safely glide on our protected pond, there is no better sight. Although they don't nest in or near our body of water, sometimes a bonded male and female will seek to "raise" their brood in our backyard. And that can be a glorious happening with many photographs taken during their short growing-up period.

Speaking of stinky and malodorous, now would be a good time to mention stink and squash bugs, yet two more "buggy gems" that gardening aficionados and homeowners often put up with. And, yes, both are true bugs – these insects have piercing/plant-juice-sucking mouthparts, and a half-wing body morphology. And although rather bulky by insect standards, both are relatively decent flyers. Large, bright green stink bugs, aka shield bugs, are frequently encountered in gardens, on berry bushes and in the home. Protected by their unusually angular shape and stout size, stink bugs also let off a noxious odor should hungry animals or curious humans attempt an assault. Of course, some birds, reptiles, amphibians, and insects eat stink bugs, but do not consume enough of them to make a dent in their widespread population. And as mentioned, they can get indoors and even overwinter, lazily clinging to windows and barely staying alive until spring comes.

Grabbing one in haste causes the emission of the telltale stench, which although not toxic, can nonetheless leave hands quite smelly. Brown-colored squash bugs are aptly named: a gardener may wish to squash those unagitated bugs that are visibly perched and virtually sucking the life out of squash plants! Like stink bugs, these elongated and relatively large insects emit a strong scent should they be mishandled or crushed. And come autumn, after the garden season is wrapped up and devoid of squash-related plants, squash bugs continue to be found in large numbers. And they can easily invade houses. Like stink bugs, they can passively *hibernate* the winter away while slowly crawling around on walls, ceilings, and floors. Though harmless, picking one up can elicit the pathognomonic stink they are famous for. I usually leave these "stinky" creatures alone whenever they are found inside the confines of our home. If, however, their presence gets overwhelming, just throw the six-legged bums out and then wash your hands. Better yet, wear gloves for that simple ordeal. The last five arthropods to be discussed are perhaps the most annoying and possibly dangerous animals that most gardeners and outdoor-loving people will encounter. Very small in stature but appearing large in disreputable circles, these mini beasts can ruin a wonderful daytime hike, an evening patio party or a leisurely stroll outside. These tiny trespassers can seemingly come out of nowhere and appear to consider mankind as either a threat or an easy source of necessary protein for reproductive purposes. Therefore, they can harm and possibly kill people. Without being too melodramatic, and as WWE wrestling superstar LA Knight would say, "Lemme talk to ya": Stinging insects - be they bees, wasps, assassin beetles, or many others - are sometimes no fun to be around. But most are content to keep their defensive stingers sheathed. However, Yellowjackets are the jerks in the crowd. Territorial and aggressive, especially in the autumn when the queen makes an overwintering home in the ground, these wasps can be more than a perturbance. Untoward anaphylactic reactions to their stings can even cause death in some predisposed individuals. As an allergic, sensitized sufferer, I had a six-year-long series of antivenin injections to supposedly treat my heightened response to Yellowjacket venom. After the completion of the therapy, I was told that I was essentially "cured." Great. But when I asked the allergist if I could return to her office someday and get a full dose shot just to see if a potent backlash occurs, I was told no. "We don't want you potentially dying here in the office," she smugly replied as if I had asked an outrageous and egregious question. Did I, though? I wanted to know if all those shots had effectively desensitized me and yet what I got in return was an eye roll and sarcastic doubletalk. Was the immunotherapy all in vain and a total scam? Probably not. It appears that the monthly jabs did do their intended job because I have unfortunately been stung numerous times by Yellowjackets over the ensuing years and have had little reactions. All good, thus far. Most of the year, omnivorous Yellowjackets are content to forage rather peacefully. However, they are highly protective of their nests, especially just before winter sets in. Guard wasps will often sting anything that moves within a few feet of the unmarked, underground nesting burrow. Oftentimes I have resorted to wearing my white, full-length bee suit when mowing my lawn, especially near the back of the property where abandoned chipmunk homes are plentiful (Yellowjackets love to usurp and use these ready-made homes). Every autumn I look like the poofy Michelin Man pushing a lawn mower, so what? Deer flies are sneaky and dreadful little monsters, and the pond most likely contributes to the large numbers found in our backyard every summer. What is it about these aerial assault-artists that make them so menacing? And as per usual in the insect world, it is the biologic FEMALES that cause humans and other animals the most misery. "Ain't it the truth? Ain't it the truth?" as The Cowardly Lion in the original *Wizard of Oz* movie once said. Because the eggs are laid on cattails and other overhanging plants near quiet bodies of fresh water, and because the larvae of these flies gestate and pupate in the muddy banks, WATER is required for their existence. Unfortunately, our puny pond unwittingly produces hordes of them. The iridescent, striped and winged womenfolk are ready to viciously bite and suck blood for their internally developing eggs; protein is needed to perpetuate the deer fly bloodline. The males, however, peacefully sip on nectar and do not have the specially designed sawing mandibles of their paramours. Some people, like Hottie Blondie, are mildly allergic to deer fly bites with painful, itchy swellings of bitten areas being the result. They can attack in swarms, with human heads, necks, and extremities being the targeted areas. Oftentimes, purposely extending an arm or elbow will induce the fly to land on it. Then it can be swatted dead! Spray-on DEET and other such insect repellents do not work well against these dogged gals. But a bonus is that they will not fly into homes or chase a human into a building, unlike mosquitos. Mosquitos, mosquitos.… I guess I am always grateful when seeing the professional exterminator truck drive by my house on its way to adjoining neighbors on my dead-end street. THEY get the "anti-mosquito" treatment and perhaps my family benefits a little as well? Maybe. I'm sure that the far-from-harmless synthetic pyrethroids indiscriminately sprayed on their respective properties not only keep THEIR mosquito populations in check, but probably waft over through the thick, tree-lined property lines and into my yard, too. All that watered-down neighborly "toxicity" undoubtedly helps, at least to a certain extent. Because on warm, humid spring nights, mosquitos become a problem for most people residing in our neck of the redneck woods. Without belaboring the point, female mosquitos are known to harbor and transmit a host of nasty and sometimes deadly diseases. Consequently, their eradication, or at least tacit management of, is always welcome. Luckily, we are not inundated with mosquitos that cause the most severe illnesses, however, Malaria, West Nile Virus, Dengue Fever, and other such ilk are slowly making northern geographical progress. Hopefully "global warming," regardless of its causation, will not turn temperate habitable zones into tropical ones and induce the spread of mosquito-borne pestilences. Although scientific literature posits that mosquitos are attracted to carbon dioxide gas exhaled by animals, it's hard to hold your breath for an extended period of time while outside. In the meantime, getting rid of small, standing pools of water and using bacterial Dunks in larger, stagnant bodies of water can be efficacious methods for local mosquito control. Fortunately, my pond has enough underwater predators to snuff out any surface-lingering mosquito eggs or larvae (wrigglers). Now on to a success story - for black flies, that is. The rapidly expanding territories of these tiny flying terrors are due in large part to water conservation methods. As the streams, brooks and culverts in our area have been cleaned up over the years, the black fly population has taken notice and migrated accordingly. Formerly an Adirondack kind of thing – Inlet, N.Y. has a yearly Black Fly Festival – most of downstate New York now has this seasonal plague, as well. They breed in fast-flowing and pristine sources of water only. Thanks a lot, EPA! Just kidding. However, these flying springtime bloodsuckers can cause bloody bites which often progress to large, itchy welts, especially in children and unwary adults. Hairlines, sock lines and most exposed skin areas are the surreptitiously targeted areas. And again, it's the females of the species that do the dastardly deeds of sneakily trying to obtain blood-meals from unwitting patsies. And like for mosquitos, DEET-containing products are the best and quickest deterrents for an unwelcome black fly that wishes to put the bite on you…. I saved the most devious for last: animals that genuinely tick me off. Ticks are eight-legged arachnids akin to spiders. They are not insects, but squeamish people often lump them into the same icky group. It doesn't really matter how they are classified or how many legs they possess: these obnoxious and secretive arthropods, and their often-painless bites, can induce acute and chronic illnesses. And these ailments, such as Lyme disease and Rocky Mountain Spotted Fever, can be extremely debilitating and last a lifetime. I should know; I have been suffering from chronic Lyme disease (Post Treatment Chronic Lyme Disease Syndrome) since 1994. Briefly, I got unknowingly bit, had widespread rashes, got a constellation of other horrible symptoms, and had to retire from work for a while. Was it Lyme disease? No one knew at the time because the primitive early Western Blot tests showed that I was Lyme negative. But I was still deathly sick. After visiting numerous well-known, infectious-disease-specializing doctors - and to no avail - in 1995 I put myself on an extended and high dose Amoxicillin antibiotic regimen. I didn't know what else to do. Modern medicine was failing me big-time (what else is new) and I strongly suspected that I had Lyme. A year later, in 1996, I finally started to come out of my terrible tailspin. I had gone from a physically fit, competitive tennis-playing, workaholic dentist and doting parent to a shell of my former self during those two intervening "lost" years. And the physiological damage had already been done. Fast forward three decades and my initial bout of Lyme disease has been corroborated by new, sophisticated tests. Yay, but many of the previous long-term symptoms have not abated to this day. Boo! It's a sucky ailment and can be contracted repeatedly, which has happened to me as well. However, taking high-dose Doxycycline within a 72-hour window after being bitten, before any telltale bullseye rash appears, is usually enough to stop the Lyme bacterium from spreading and causing bodily harm. But not all ticks carry the "bad" bacteria. Nevertheless, taking the correct antibiotic is prudent assurance that the disease will hopefully not manifest itself. And if it does, usually first as an unexplained rash, taking a custom-designed Doxycycline regimen (other antibiotics can also be used) for at least a two-week course will generally knock it out. Of course, there are many types of infections that ticks can carry and pass on to animals and humans, Lyme being only one of them. But enough about me – ha, ha! Juvenile female and male ticks, through blood-feeding on infected mice and deer, ingest transmittable viruses, bacteria, and parasites. These disease-causing microbes are then in turn passively passed into the bloodstreams of humans and other animals by the blood-sucking adult ticks, mainly the egg-laying females. Ticks are hard-boiled life-forms. They are able to withstand widely fluctuating temperatures, drought, rainy conditions, and lack of food. Flattened and hard to squash, they are a tribute to one of nature's miniscule creatures that are tough to kill. To obtain nourishment, most ticks climb out onto the very edges of vegetation with outstretched claws (questing) and hope for an unwary passerby to rub against them. Then they quickly latch onto the host and begin gently and slowly climbing around until finding a non-hairy area to bite. Recent literature states that they also have a static electrical potential which aids them in their ability to gravitate toward other objects. This unique feature may give them a leg up to grab onto living things. As I mow with my lawn tractor, I inadvertently brush up against lots of vegetation and pine tree needles. That's most likely how I messed up years ago, and continually invite trouble. And lack of a head-to-toe bodycheck afterwards often prevents outdoorsmen (and women) from visualizing any sesame-seed-sized cretins crawling on their respective skins. Although, sometimes you CAN feel them, especially in tight areas such as beneath underwear bands and under socks. Wearing light colored clothing, tucking in socks and shirts, and discarding or thoroughly washing outdoor-worn clothing can help in seeing the little troublemakers and preventing any ingress for bloodletting purposes, respectively. Hopefully, I have not dissuaded anyone from any horticultural pursuits due to my sordid depictions of naturally occurring wild animals, both large and small. However, furry, winged and hard-shelled buggers that continually want to fuck with me are dealing with an intelligent and ill-tempered old goat

(Not G.O.A.T). A person that is willing to put up with only so much gardening-related crapola before lashing out with unrepeatable words and feeble warnings to all the "guilty" birds, beasts and bugs out there. Oh, well, we are all in this together, I guess.

20

Grass Clippings

Mulch, mulch, and mulch some more. That seems to be the unspoken mantra in gardening circles. And grass clippings, though unsightly when used to encircle berry bushes and ornamental plants, tend to work beautifully when placed between rows of veggies for moisture retention, nutrient sequestration, and weed blocking. What's not to love about grass (and not the kind you smoke)? However, I have largely abandoned the use of clippings in lieu of straight-up hand weeding (hoeing or literally pulling weeds by hand) or with straw placement. Anyway, years ago I could have let my "natural" grassy lawn grow tall and then cut and rake it specifically for the largesse (Yeah right. I keep it shaved at precisely three inches high), but I chose an easier method instead. My policeman neighbor would always dump huge mounds of his unwanted, freshly cut grass in the corner of our dead-end street's cul-de-sac edges. It was easy for me to hitch my trusty wagon to one of my lawn tractors and transport the prize home. The neighbor did not mind, and our mutual street looked neater after I was done collecting the shredded bonanza. It took just a few trips, and I was all set to distribute the green-colored goodness up and down my rows of veggies.

But wait, what was that strange truck doing on our street? The one that advertised itself as a lawn-care specialist. Uh oh. Now there were tiny yellow flags planted all over my neighbor's yard, ones with a skull and crossbones logo on them. I assumed that the lawn service used potent herbicides (potentially poisonous to humans) to kill clover, crabgrass, etc. Had this outfit come before? And for how long had the cop been employing them? Perhaps the grass (his grass) that I now had in my garden was contaminated with cancer-causing chemicals. Rats! Yet here I was cavalierly spreading it around as if it was green gold. Obviously, I instantly stopped using foreign grass clippings and started procuring my own. That neighbor eventually did tell me that he only recently started using various "lawn doctors" and that I should be okay with the old stuff. Wow! Please be careful and find out beforehand from whence seemingly innocous botanical offshoots come from. Lesson learned. Hopefully not the hard way.

21

Rain Barrels, or Not

Having them was "big" in the nineties as part of a natural gardening experience whereby "organic" rainwater would be utilized for watering the garden and other plants. You know, a holistic approach for using nature's bounties instead of tapping into tap or well water. And I was guilty of purchasing three large rain barrels from a big box gardening outfit, affixing them to the downspouts of my house gutters, and felt all set. I would now have hundreds of gallons at my disposal, water that could also be used for drinking - in a dire pinch of course! What a misguided moron I was. To make a long story even shorter, and I'm almost finished now, the fanciful notion of gathering and distributing freely acquired liquid gold to thirsty plants never really materialized. A big, fat goose egg! What happened? Well, firstly, unused rainwater during times of weather-wetness just sat there and quickly became visibly contaminated. And the possibility of adding chlorine or other chemicals to the barrels was antithetical to the whole process. Of course, periodically draining the said containers to avoid "watery infection" would also deplete the reserves that I had sought to accumulate. Well, that was one thing. Another problem was the release of the water from the green, plastic kegs. Unusually small and difficult-to-manage drain hoses at the very bottoms of the barrels made filling up watering containers an arduous task. And one more dilemma: removing and storing the big vats during winters was a non-starter. They were heavy as hell as it was, and any remaining water in them only multiplied their weight. However, leaving them out through the cold season caused the leftover water inside to freeze and crack the plastic drain holes and even ruin the exterior plastic shells. In summary, either I was not fastidious enough to properly care for these no-brainer gardening aids, or they were a pain in the ass that only looked good on paper. Maybe both are true. After a few years of trying to make repository rainwater tanks work for and not against me, I got rid of them. We still have periods of dry summer weather and I reminisce about those barrels being full of water and ready to help me out. But then I recall the frustrations involved in their usage as I fill up my buckets with hard, iron and sulfur-infused well water. Oh, well.

22

Topiary Scientist?

Starting in ancient Roman times, topiary is the art and science of willfully shaping perennial trees and shrubbery by clipping the foliage. It sounds easy, but you CAN severely damage or exterminate the plant by overcutting it for the sake of artistic expression, hence the science part of it. The art part is the seemingly endless variety of possible shapes that can be achieved using a wide range of plants, mainly dense-leafed shrubs. Much like ice and wooden log sculptures, creative topiary involves the use of specially designed pruning and cutting hand-tools. However, often the bush in question has to be slowly - and I mean slowly - "trained" into its final shapeliness by years of judicious cuts. Sometimes, the branches initially need to be coaxed into certain positions, held in place for a while and then allowed to grow before any surface foliage clipping can be done. Unlike static objects, such as ice and wood, most living leafy twigs cannot be severely manipulated or sheared into shape and expected to survive and thrive. Of course, some bushes are more amenable than others for their abilities to "take a licking and keep on ticking" (phrase lifted from an old Timex watch commercial). However, my extensive foray into topiary largely consists of horizontally trimming arborvitae and Privet hedges, and vertically edging the sides of my property: the encroaching pruned plants range from deciduous trees to vines and even poison ivy - and everything in between! After excitedly purchasing two different-sized power-trimmers and a bunch of handheld scissors, pruners and bladed cutters, I was all set to "artfully" tackle my three-acre property and keep the various plants from overwhelming my land and sense of pride. But I wasn't forced into this position of servitude to the lawn and surrounding greenery. After all, I'm the one who planted most of the stuff in and around my large yard in the first place. And now I had to take care of it. I could have just let things grow willy-nilly… nah, nah, not on my watch! Anyway, this is where my wife and I frequently butt heads. She loves to admire mature shrubs with all their vibrant finery intact, not realizing that they are getting taller with only the top and side parts producing the leaves. Constant "shaping" is required to carefully leave a modicum of "green" while reducing the size slightly to keep things in check. But she hates the newly cut plants. "What's the point of having ornamental bushes if you continually scalp them?" she often laments while staring crossly at me. "But if I let them grow and then cut them back to their original sizes, there will only be branches to gaze at," I frequently counter. "And then they would all most likely die," I ruefully add for emphasis. Well, this kind of banter continues every summer with no abatement in sight. Of course, it was the sweet spot that I was always looking for whenever trimming: how to make it look like I did nothing while preventing the shrubs from getting out of control. That is the horticultural dilemma I always face. Wait a second. Perhaps I should let my wife handle the time consuming and physical horticultural chores around our extensive yard and see how she does? Maybe, but I don't want to do things over after she is done! Sorry. Years ago, and knowing my perfectionist-type personality, my two young children would sometimes rush into the house and tease me after I finished a long and tiring session of pruning - right after I removed my ensemble of hat, safety glasses, boots, and Kevlar-lined, cut-proof gloves. "Hey Dad," my smart aleck son would exclaim, "I think you missed more than a few spots." "Hey Dad, that plant you just cut is growing again," my smart-ass daughter would gleefully add. And then my observant wife would fold her arms and contribute her two cents…. What a bunch of maroons, but I love them just the same. But I am NO topiary scientist. Nevertheless, at least there are no vines creeping into our domicile; thirty-plus years later and my wife and I can still see out our front windows and over the tops of the meticulously trimmed bushes that I continually give haircuts to. By the way, and quite quizzically, all that attention given to coifing wayward leaves does seem to have a pastoral, calming effect on me. All's well.

23

Stopping the Rot

I find it amusing whenever I hear a television play-by-play announcer of British origin matter-of-factly state that a tennis player has "stopped the rot." It means that a prolonged losing streak has finally ended. English colloquialisms are sometimes a hoot to hear, especially when you least expect them. However, I am NOT amused when it comes to unsuccessfully stopping the rot on my Ukrainian quince tree! Quince is a deciduous tree and produces aromatic, HARD, tart, yellow-colored fruit. Although related to apples and pears, don't try to bite into one unless you have jaws and teeth made of steel. My quince stands right next to the peach tree, and you would think that wild animals, such as possums, would rightly eat the fruit of both. But no. Ripe peaches are usually ravaged while the big, beautiful, golden-hued pomes of the quince are untouched by rogue teeth. And I mean untouched. Not a mark to be found. I guess even a marauding furry mammal does not relish broken choppers. But the hardy and productive quince suffers from a malady that is difficult to eradicate: brown rot. This fungus frequently infects all "stone fruit," however our peaches have never been affected. Most of our extensive, yearly quince crop is thrown away because of this fungal disease. It is an unfortunate waste of fruit. Even during early summer some of the leaves start turning brown, indicating trouble ahead. And while most of the growing fruit looks edible on the surface, in fact, some of the hanging quince already have the rot inside. Picking off the slowly discoloring leaves and pruning the cankered branches and brown-spotted fruits in late summer seem to help prevent the spread of the ailment. But once it hits, the brown, spongy and powdery mass of fungus envelopes the individual fruits causing many to fall off prematurely. Yellowjackets and other insects just love this messy smorgasbord under my tree, diving deep into the softened and damaged fruits to get their nourishment. Covering the trees in early spring with tea or Neem oil MAY be a productive endeavor, but I have not found it to be so. "Organic" copper and sulfur-based sprays are touted as being effective if applied after blossoming. Maybe. Spraying trees with a potent fungicide is yet another way to potentially save the fruit. But the commercially available antifungals have different levels of toxicity, and some cannot be directly applied to the ripened fruits without the possibility of harming humans. It is a tough seasonal situation and, because no chemical means are used as preventatives, I expect a large loss. But the "clean" bushel that is picked every October becomes a prized commodity. These fruits are greatly appreciated for their tangy flavor. And although most types of quinces cannot be eaten raw, they are high in pectin and make delectable jams, jellies and sauces. Pies are another avenue for quince to grace. In our home, my wife peels and grates the fruit before boiling the shavings with MUCH added sugar to cut the tartness. Prolonged cooking with sugar turns the flesh of the pale fruit red due to the presence of pigmented anthocyanins. The resultant and different canned products are stored and eaten all winter. My favorite are the light-tasting sauces and not the thick jams. However, in other parts of the world, quince is routinely added to a variety of foods, such as applesauce. Additionally, alcoholic drinks, meads, marmalades, and even cheeses can be made with quince as a main ingredient. But, to each her own.

24

Peaches and Herbs

I couldn't resist ripping off and adulterating that seminal name just to find an adequate title with which to describe my lone peach tree and my wife's herb garden. Peaches and Herb, a still popular R & B, soul, funk, and disco-singing duo would be pleased. Or not! Most likely the latter…. Anyway, let's begin with the peach tree, which stands regally in my carefully curated backyard. Come rain or shine, winter and summer, it has been a constant presence for the last two decades. However, though it has shown bravery through gales, searing and subzero temperatures, climate change (I had to throw that in for fun), and a host of leaf and fruit-eating varmints, it is down to only one large branch. Sadly, the rest of the limbs have been pruned away in increments due to dry rot and death. It is barely alive at this point and while continually pushing out leaves, it is no longer producing fruit. But it is part of our horticultural family dammit, and I will nurse it until it fully succumbs. Will I plant another one? I doubt it. But not because I am so emotionally attached to this one; another major factor is at play. Digressing a bit, peach trees live for 7 to 15 years. We got much more life out of it than we bargained for, however, peaches were not produced during most of those years. In addition, being of dwarf stock may also have contributed to its seemingly shortened lifespan and inconsistent production, although twenty years is darn good for any fruit tree. The main reason for not planting another one is opossums. Yes, these short-lived (up to two years) American marsupials are harmless to humans, but a menace when it comes to persimmons, nectarines, and peaches. And since I only have one peach tree, any time it was loaded with ripe, aromatic, and tasty peaches most, it not all, were quickly polished off nocturnally. Finding and kicking around the gnawed and gnarled pits on the ground after such nightly binges was both frustrating and disappointing. There weren't that many hanging fruits there to begin with, and MY watering mouth wanted to eat them! Sure, a few times I caught the persistent possums in the act. So what. After I chased them away, they always returned, and not to play dead, but to feed on fresh, fruity produce directly at the source and right in my yard! Anyhow, every few years, whenever the tree DECIDED to be fruitful and multiplied, and if I somehow outfoxed the opossums, my family and I would be blessed with a large bushel of beautiful peaches. Either I beat the possums to the prize, or they simply were not around during that particular harvest season. I don't know what happened. Needless to say, I will be saddened when our peach tree finally bites the dust. Moving along - an herb garden sounds so enticing, old-fashioned, New Age and holistic. And it can be. Unfortunately, it can also quickly become a nightmare with "uncooperative," facile plants that did not get the message for slow growth and non-proliferation. My wife "runs" the smallish, triangular patch which is situated adjacent to our concrete back porch and borders a row of arborvitae bushes as well as a brick patio. It is basically enclosed, however, it has a mind of its own and WANTS to get out of hand. Every November she dutifully adds mulch and puts it to bed. In the spring, like clockwork, she tirelessly preps, re-mulches, and conditions the soil for the usual assortment of anticipated bay leaf plants, lavender, sage, rosemary, bee balm, etc. You know, a bunch of eclectic annuals and perennials which can be picked, dried, and used as garnishes and spices. However, years ago the newly growing mint and thyme plants really got out of control, causing Hottie Blondie great consternation and displeasure. At first it seemed simple: stick in just a FEW mint and thyme plants to enjoy their adult greenery for flavored water and desiccated leaves for teas and cakes. However, the few paltry plants spread quickly, and in a few seasons overwhelmed the whole lot. The thyme, though a circular woody herb and cover for rabbits, somehow escaped the loose borders of its confinement and invaded my grassy back yard. Now there are large spots of dark green thyme living and growing in my backyard, but not by choice. However, since I do not use any herbicides or chemicals to either enhance or alter my lawn's vegetative residents, thyme will continue to slowly spread. At a glance, it looks as though my lawn is suffering from the "Heartbreak of Psoriasis," with no cure in sight. Mint and thyme, what a disastrous duo they turned out to be. However, ever the industrious gardener, Hottie Blondie extirpated ALL the mint plants, and weed-killed any new growths. She also brutally cut back the thyme, and any undesirable new shoots. She left it as a small bush, eyeing it periodically in case it starts to spread. And she was able to reclaim her prized herb garden. Amen to that! I was not so lucky in my endeavor with the lawn thyme. I tried to physically remove it by digging it up. Like dealing with cancer, total marginal removal is ideal. But I could not reconcile obliterating HUGE swaths of lawn, adding topsoil, and reseeding. And thyme roots are not shallow, darn it. So, I didn't do that. Weed killing was not an option either, because it would leave many uneven and denuded tracts behind. Then I would have to dig up the poison-treated areas, truck in more topsoil, and reseed…. So, the thyme won. I can smell the cuttings when I mow over it. It's not unpleasant, but it reminds me of my failure as an amateur "organic" landscaper. Now, I'm sure if I hired a professional lawn service, and with the use of chemical know-how, my lawn would be the envy of many. However, I prefer to keep it natural. As my old man used to say, "It's OK, as long as it's some kind of green."

25

Mounds?

It's often a point of contention and confrontation between some home-gardeners. Not with MY kin, but in good, wholesome, and astute families who plant gardens together. At least that's what I've heard. Or maybe I heard wrong and am just winding people up with contrived innuendos, manufactured gossip, and phony outrage? Just like the divisive drivel emanating from the odious major TV "news" networks? Possibly. Anyway, is a foot-high mound of soil preferred for favorable growth of certain veggies or were the Native Americans and even earlier Meso-American cultures who practiced this form of agriculture woefully and agriculturally naïve? Of course, those ancient peoples WERE known for successfully raising the "three sisters," namely maize (corn), pole beans, and squash. The corn was planted first in the middle of the miniscule hill, the bean seeds next to the kernels, and then the squash, which surrounded the mounds. The climbing bean plants (legumes) provided "fixed nitrogen" for optimal growth, meaning that certain bacteria take gaseous nitrogen from the air and in turn feed this gas to the bean roots. In exchange, the plant provides carbohydrates to the bacteria. Additionally, the beans used the corn stalks as a natural trellis, thereby helping themselves to grow while stabilizing the corn from possible wind damage. The encircling squash plants acted as protective soil covers to impede the growth of undesirable weeds and to keep the moisture constant at the base of the tiny hillocks. I guess the indigenous peoples didn't starve, received most of their protein from plants, and basically knew what they were doing after all. However, without the corn and beans as adjutants, should squash and zucchini be planted in mini hills, too? Or is "flat" the way to go? These are the kinds of diametrically opposed arguments that can get a mild-mannered gardener's dandruff up in a Goddamn hurry. Good Lord - growing vegetables was supposed to be fun and free of controversy. Yeah, right! Let's briefly explore: my wife and I have tried it both ways, hilled and flat-top. We have found that each has pluses and minuses. A mound induces pinnacle-placed squash and zucchini to grow more vigorously because nutritious topsoil is concentrated in the hunched-up dirt, not to mention the effects of gravity. And this is true for melons and pumpkins, too. They are literally growing downhill, down the sides of the earthen hump. However, in times of drought, extra watering is necessary because not only are these types of plants heavy drinkers but any remaining liquid in the mound tends to seep south. Flat-growing works just fine, except during times of excess wetness. Unplanned and prolonged rain showers can readily flood a garden or at least make it soggy-boggy for a while. This can easily induce rot in the spiky, skin-sensitizing leaves, stems, flowering ends, and oblong fruits (yes, squash and the related zucchini are technically fruits) unless the water drains away quickly or there is adequate absorbent straw underneath the plants. So, there you have it. During the last few seasons, the Wife and I have nixed the mounds and still gotten volumes of tasty squash and zucchini. Now the only *Mounds* we enjoy are made by Hershey.

26

Cukes

No casual gardening conversation would be complete without the mention of the ubiquitous cucumbers. It's as if everyone grows them, or at least pretends to. Much lip service is paid to this elongated, slightly spiky veggie and its pickled end-product – the gherkin. Although in the U.S., pickled cucumbers are generally called pickles. Mom would pick ripe, fresh cukes from our garden, wash them and scrub off the bristles, cut off both ends, slice them into two halves lengthwise, sprinkle table salt on both cut surfaces, rub the salted halves against each other, and serve them as crunchy appetizers before dinner. Yummo! Of course, many experienced gardeners and cooks do this. I'm not sure if she knew that she was basically removing some of the cucumber's cucurbitacins (tetracyclic triterpenoids for all you organic chemists out there), which are protective bitter chemicals concentrated in the ends to help prevent the gourd from being eaten in the wild. But, after rubbing, my mom did not rinse off the whitish, foamy substance that formed on both cut halves like some knowledgeable people do. But I never complained or knew anything different. I thought all cucumbers had a slightly bitter aftertaste, like bad beer (I should know), and learned to be keen on it. An acquired taste, I guess. Today, my favorite way to prepare them is to first wash the cukes and knock off the spicules, cut them crosswise, and then eat the thin slices with a dollop of ranch dressing. My wife likes to wash and peel 'em, cut them crosswise, and then coat the pieces in a sauce made of freshly squeezed lemon juice and mayo before enjoying the tangy treats. Cucumbers may appear to be dull and boring, however, they have a rich history and can be devoured raw, cooked, or pickled. Let's find out more about these dour dildoes of the garden. Technically, cucumbers are creeping vines and, with spiraling tendrils that seem to have "eyes," try to climb onto and encircle anything in their paths. Always thirsty for water, the large, ragged-looking, green leaves often wilt on hot days indicating that they are parched, and the roots need a drink. The entire sprawling plant, stems and fruit included, is festooned with miniature spiky protuberances. Although these tiny, sharp "hairs" do not thwart the average human gardener, they may be a deterrent to some animals. And again, most peeps call them veggies, but based on flowering and biological parameters, they are rightfully fruits. Although strictly speaking, the lowly cucumber is classified as a *pepo*, a type of botanical berry. Good grief! Anyway, there are three major cultivars: burpless, pickling, and slicing. All three types seemed to have originated in different parts of the world, from ancient India and East Asia to the classical Greek and Roman periods of yesteryear. Modern North American varieties were brought over by early Spanish explorers and incorporated by the indigenous tribes into their agricultural pursuits. In all, cucumbers have been brined, pickled, sliced, diced, and dined on by a host of human cultures throughout history. As an aside, the manual Veg-O-Matic food chopper of the '70s did a magnificent job cutting most vegetables. It was a popular kitchen item at the time and showcased how easy it was to prepare veggies for dinner, including cucumbers. I like to plant the usual dark-green, seedless types, although I have experimented with smooth, yellow-skinned, and even striped varieties. The seeds and plantings available are seemingly endless, with most greenhouses being a major purveyor of seedlings in the spring. Without being too verbose, or to overly extoll the virtues of this common garden plant, suffice it to say that a few things have to occur for a successful cucumber crop: an initial enclosure to prevent chipmunks, rabbits, and woodchucks from sawing off the tender baby leaves (which often kills the plant and you have to start over and replant), LOTS of water to keep the roots hydrated, adequate insect (mainly honeybee and bumblebee) pollination, and a favorable environment in which to grow. We grow our triplet seedlings with a surrounding bed of straw in close proximity to tomato plants. Why tomatoes? Well, they are vertically growing plants tethered to steel posts and, being tall and leafy, create lots of necessary shade for the grateful cucumbers below. Also, the tomatoes act as natural scaffolding for the climbing potential of the cucumber plants. Although I generally do not allow them to wholly take over the tomatoes, it's a balancing act between these two plants and the wishes of the gardener. But I DO allow the cucumber vines and stems to encircle the tomato stalks in a serpentine, ground-level manner as the tendrils try desperately to latch onto something. Every year we try a few different varieties that we have never grown before and are never disappointed. The reward is rapidly growing hybridized greenery composed of twisty stems covered by angular leaves and yellow flowers. All of that vegetative growth culminates in the production of delicious cukes, many of which try to stay hidden under their extensive and cooling leaf cover. It's always surprising to "find" a gigantic one that was not spotted and picked earlier. Cucumber popularity has waxed and waned throughout recorded time: from initially being cheered by early civilizations, then vilified as only fit for cows in the 17th century, to once more gracing many gardens and kitchen tables; and found as pickles in most grocery stores and gourmet shops. They are literally

everywhere and consumed by nearly everybody in one
form or another. To quote the catchy slogan of
Virginia Slims cigarettes: "You've come a long way,
baby!"

27

Hornworm Horror

Our tomato plants didn't produce bountiful harvests year after year. That being said, there was one season when Mother Nature piled on to completely ruin an already niggardly crop. What the eff? Thanks a lot. And the miscreants she sent to finish the job were tomato hornworms! And boy, was I chagrined. After all, I fancy myself an amateur entomologist and should have noticed them well before they annihilated the already stressed plants. Well, I'm being overly dramatic but, still, it's always something as "they" say. The horned caterpillar onslaught is yet another variable to consider when trying to successfully raise tomatoes. But let's examine "love-apples" in general before we *circle back* (I love that facetious two-word reply that former, fake-orange-haired and pretentious press secretary Jen Psaki used to say) and discuss those diabolical insect larvae proper. Tomatl and Xitomatl (ancient Aztec), Tomate (Spanish), Poms, Golden Apples, "Wolf Apples," "Wolf Peach," and other regionally derived nomenclature all refer to the tomato plant, a botanical berry (fruit) that is generally considered a vegetable. Most horticultural authorities agree that this plant was originally grown for food by various

Meso-American cultures, such as the Aztecs, before the Spanish conquistadors exported the plants to all their Caribbean, European, far-Eastern, and South American holdings. The fruits started out no larger than blueberries and were intentionally bred to have various colors, shapes, sizes, textures, and flavors. Viral, fungal, and bacterial resistance and extended shelf life then became modern hallmarks of this highly manipulated plant. However, some knowledgeable botanists will say that all the genetic tinkering required to produce long-lasting, visually pleasing, disease-free specimens has resulted in most commercially grown tomatoes being rather bland and thick skinned. Not exactly an inspiring addition to the supper table. And even the home-grown garden varieties, both heirloom (grown for over forty years without hybridization) and hybrids, are a far cry from the intensely sweet and tasty tomatoes of ancient times. At least, that's what the history books imply. Anyhow, tomatoes are technically vines which are trained to grow vertically by most gardeners. And they are prolific growers. Trimming the ends of this usually annual flora merely induces the plant to branch off lateral stems before flowering occurs. And though the greenery can be eaten, it is advisable not to. Being a member of the "deadly" nightshade family of plants, the tomato leaves – and green, unripe tomatoes - contain the natural toxins called solanines and chaconine. Though poisonous, the amounts found are small and generally inconsequential if eaten in small quantities. Okay, so what do WE grow and eat? Hottie Blondie either starts the indoor process from seeds (in late March or early April) or purchases already potted, greenhouse-started seedlings in late May. She has done both in one season, but more often than not, does one or the other. The advantage of seeds is that you can purchase most any variety out there, culture them indoors, and then transplant them to the garden. However, most of the seedlings die and large amounts of seeds are wasted. The greenhouse-bought plants are usually hardy and ready to go, but the various types for sale are often limited. And popular varieties are quickly sold out. Of course, we could buy exotic heirloom potted tomatoes from mail-order companies found around the world, but there is no telling if they would successfully grow or yield in our part of Upstate New York. American Oxheart, Brandywine, Cherry, and San Marzano are our preferred heirloom tomatoes. However, "life happens," and we don't always follow through on starry-eyed, wintry decisions. Poorly timed vacations, inclement springtime weather, local greenhouse availability, and sometimes emerging in the spring as work-shy and bone-idle *schlubs* after a somnolent and depressing winter can have an influence on what we ultimately deposit in the dirt, especially when it comes to tomatoes. Without insulting the intelligence of fellow gardeners by pontificating about the above-mentioned four varieties, suffice it to say that the large, "sweet," salmon-skinned, flavor-packed and meaty Brandywine heirlooms are the favorites in our household. With big potato-leaved foliage, they are the "best." However, for reasons already mentioned, we don't always plant them and, sadly, it is our loss. San Marzanos (originally cultivated and still famous in the area between Salerno and Naples, Italy) are similar to oblong Roma tomatoes but are pointier and thinner skinned. The flavor is robust, with just the right amount of acidity. And the fruits have thick, firm, light red flesh. The outsides can be orange or red; they are juicy but not watery and make outstanding sauces. Cherry tomatoes are a delight to grow and gulp, and the yield per plant can be substantial. However, a common problem is the splitting that may occur right when they are ripening, especially after a hard rain when the water is rapidly absorbed through the roots. Otherwise, they are a treat. Lastly is the American Oxheart. Although finicky and prone to blight and rot, much like the Brandywine, this large tomato is the *bomb*. However, it can be difficult to find a totally unblemished specimen when it is ready to be picked. But they are fantastic when sliced and put into sandwiches! Now don't get me started about other tomato types that we sometimes reluctantly raise whenever our four favorites are not available. Big Boy, Early Girl, Girlie Man, Beefsteak, Trans Boy, etc., are somehow very popular varieties in our area. Even the huge box stores sell them as seedlings and young plants. But, why? In my opinion, they all suck! And don't let the ostentatious names fool you. Frequently poor growth, as well as small and tasteless tomatoes, are what I have personally witnessed time and again. However, we still buy them now and then when the preferred others are not at hand. All right, now it's time to grow some tomatoes! Come late May, either nursery-bought plantings or self-started seedlings are poked into the previously rototilled and smoothed out garden bed, but not before Hottie Blondie fully prepares the dug-out areas that will receive the plants. Using a specialized pharmaceutical mixing technique in a large metal bowl, my retired pharmacist wife concocts a "dirty confection" composed of sugar, manure, Epsom salts, Miracle-Gro powder and a few additional ingredients that even I am not privy to, and carefully spades them into the holes. Then she gently places the juvenile tomato plantings into their new homes and tamps down the soil around them. I follow suit by hammering in five-foot-tall metal rebars adjacent to each tomato; these are used to train and tie the plants to as they grow upwards. But why employ metal rods? Why not use sticks or long wooden stakes? Well, steel is obviously stronger and although it will corrode a little, metal will outlast buried wood which tends to rot when buried in the ground. I have reused my metal rods for close to thirty years. While they have a little surface rust on them, they are still more than functional. Another reason to use metallic stakes with nylon (from pantyhose) ties is more anecdotal in nature. I have heard this in gardening circles for years, namely, that lightning storms cause an ionic disturbance in the atmospheric, life-force energy field (oh no, not Star Wars and Reiki jargon!) at ground level. It seems that the metal and nylon (static electricity potential) bindings transmit this so-called electrical energy to the tomato plants which helps them grow. Now, whether this is fact, hearsay, or hokum is hard to tell. My Grandpa Pete, the old-school agricultural wizard from Estonia insisted it was true, at least the metal rod part. However, though I employ metal posts, I use cut-up old shirts as the ties that bind. Perhaps I should go to nylon? I don't know. My wife doesn't really wear hosiery so there are no discarded pairs available for me to dissect. And her stretchy yoga pants don't seem to wear out…. Some avid gardeners use metal cages, instead. Unfortunately, I remember that mine toppled over and frequently entangled the growing tomato plant making these popular structures more of a nuisance than an aid. I stopped using them decades ago. Of course, if you intentionally grow small tomatoes then funnel-shaped, wire enclosures may be appropriate. Curating our twenty or so plants is important. I lop the tops off the plants when they exceed the height of the poles they are attached to. This seems to give me larger fruit, although I am sacrificing additional flowering blossoms and possibly more tomatoes. My wife routinely clips off the suckers near the bottom of each plant to help prevent verticillium rot and encourage more energy be spent on the tomatoes produced. Management is key; we cut the tops and suckers and keep the vine growing vertically to prevent the fragile and disease-prone fruits and leaves from touching the soil surface. As far as problems go, there are virtually scores of viral, bacterial, and fungal illnesses that can befall the tomato. In addition, there are lots of insect pests and outside forces that can also damage these plants. Verticillium blight is caused by a fungus and spreads mainly underground from root to root; more readily if the roots are even slightly abraded such as by their climbing over an underground rock. It's important not to place any stakes too close to the young rootlets so as not to inadvertently damage them and provide an ingress point for the verticillium. The fungus gets into the xylem water channels (remember high school biology class?) and the infection spreads everywhere, although in tomatoes the bottom rungs of the plant seem to be affected first. And this persistent pestilence can stay alive in the soil for many years. Some solutions for rearing fungi-free tomatoes include the following: rotation of crops, picking off afflicted leaves, and the planting of hardier, disease-resistant cultivars. Sometimes commercial farms will resort to chemical fumigation of the soil, but permits are required, and it can be a laborious and expensive process. All in all, once a plant becomes internally infected it cannot be externally saved, only managed. Leaves turn yellow, then brown, and finally wilt and fall off. However, many fruits can still be salvaged as the plant gradually dies from the slow-growing fungus. Blossom end rot is another baddy, especially when it comes to San Marzano tomatoes. It is an affliction manifested by the appearance of sunken brown and leathery patches, that eventually turn black and rot, which are found on the blossom ends of affected tomatoes. The tomatoes may look healthy, and then – wham, blossom end rot! Sometimes while closely examining and fondling them, much like during a testicular exam, the diseased fruit will fall off the vine. It is frustrating to see one after another San Marzano masterpiece go to waste. But what exactly causes this scourge? Many gardening pundits flippantly seem to think that it is merely a physiological phenomenon due to a lack of soil calcium. However, some horticulturists insist that other factors are responsible, notably, irregular watering or too much available ground nitrogen and magnesium. I am not a botanist, in fact I am barely a legal gardener, but I will say that even after "correcting" the above-mentioned mineral levels, mulching, and properly watering my charge, I still sometimes get blossom end rot. And it always hits the San Marzano tomatoes more often than the other varieties. I guess I'm still doing something wrong. And now, after taking this convoluted and bloviated detour to talk about tomatoes in general, let's get back on track and describe the hornworm horror that befell me. There are numerous exogenous foes besides insects, including mites and slugs, that can severely damage tomato foliage. And when it comes to young plants, that can be devastating or even terminal. But in my estimation, the Tomato Hornworm wins the prize for its sheer brazenness to chew down tomato plants while leaving the fruit alone. One early summer day I was NOT minding my own business and happened to notice something moving in one of my spindly and already struggling Brandywine tomato plants. Upon closer inspection, I was horrified by what I saw. There were at least six or seven, four-inch-long and one-inch-thick, soft, smooth, white striped, spiracled (those holes along their sides that caterpillars passively breathe with — ones that loosely resemble the decorative vent-holes found on the front fenders of old Buicks) and red-tailed, green larva contentedly munching away and pooping frass like no one was watching. Except I was, and I became hopping mad. Not only was I angry with these wayward caterpillar behemoths devouring MY tomato plants, but I was greatly disappointed as well. I consider myself a shrewd gardener and yet, I had miserably failed to watch over and protect my meager fruits. I glanced around and realized that every single tied-up tomato vine was "infected" by these hungry worms. Well, after the niggling shock wore off, I calmly picked all of them off by hand and placed them into a small bucket. Then I stood there reminiscing while watching the forty or so caterpillars wriggle over each other at the bottom of the plastic pail. As a young naturalist, I had handled them in the many gardens that I ventured through during my "buggy" collecting forays. Back then, I actively sought out the pleasure and privilege to barehandedly hold "snakes, slugs, spiders and salamanders." And it still is. Some unsophisticated and possibly unsanitary habits die hard. Anyway, after I snapped out of my brief remembrance, I noticed the extensive damage that was inflicted on my already haggard and sapped plants. After this onslaught, most of the plants looked barely alive and would probably not produce much produce. There must have been many pregnant female hornworm moths in the area to have laid so many eggs on so many plants. Anyhow, the nocturnal adult moths (Manduca quinquemaculata) sip nectar while the young stuff themselves with leaves from the Solanaceae family. This includes tomatoes, eggplants, peppers, potatoes, and tobacco. The female lays eggs on leaves near the stems of the plants. After hatching, the camouflaged juvenile eating machines usually dine at night before becoming larger and braver, and then eventually venture out to the tips of the leaves in broad daylight. Birds, mammals and parasitic wasps prey on them, although the caterpillar coloration makes finding them a difficult task. The tobacco hornworm is a close cousin and obviously eats tobacco leaves. Commercial growers of tobacco use biological controls as well as traps to keep the "Marlboro producing" leaves from being ingested. The best advice for gardeners like me is to do what I did, namely, pick them off and destroy the lot before they have a chance to burrow into the dirt, pupate and then emerge as adults the following spring to start the cycle over again. However, being the bug lover that I am, I decided to spare the collected hornworms instead. I took the mature caterpillars to my office and within a week managed to give them all away – each one was ensconced inside a Ziploc bag poked with air holes – to young, nature-loving dental patients. I instructed each budding naturalist on how to handle the caterpillars without killing them. Then

I suggested that each put a layer of loose dirt in a small plastic terrarium, plop the "worm" inside and watch the pupation process unfold. And, if all went well, the reward next spring would be a large moth in the container; a magnificently winged specimen that could be held, studied, or even pinned. As a child and adolescent, I used to collect multitudes of butterfly and moth larvae while on many entomological excursions. It was always great fun to be part of insect metamorphoses, if only as an observer. However, fast forward a few decades and that one year saw me lose a boatload of tomato plants due to crappy growing conditions and hornworms. The naughty caterpillars ended up being the coup de grâce on top of an already subpar gardening season. But at least many curious children got to play with them and hopefully learned some naturalistic principles in the process.

28

ASS-paragus

I usually don't swear unless greatly provoked. However, my derelict row of asparagus plants frequently provokes me into cussing out loud! They do this by purposely underperforming, even after being cared for with utmost agricultural acumen. I am always taken aback by the poor return on investment during some years; that kind of perceived insult makes me want to explode in indignation. Let me explain: my asparagus are assholes, plain and simple. They have every opportunity to excel at growing and to give me munchable greens, but instead seem to have developed an obstinate and arrogant attitude. Their unwillingness to put out is a frustrating tease and would raise the hackles of any hungry horticulturist. I expect my asparagus plants to flourish yearly and reward me with bountiful yields. After all, they were properly planted over a decade ago and ALWAYS receive the "TLC" treatment. Give me a break! What the hell is going on here? Approximately ten years ago, and after much online learning, I thought I was finally prepared to launch a bona fide foray into growing delicious asparagus. In the spring, I meticulously got the weed-free, twenty-foot-long by two-foot-wide bed ready and felt confident enough to order at least twenty crowns. It would be a labor of prolonged love because it usually takes a few years for the asparagus plants to become fully mature and edible. The spider-resembling, withered crowns came in. I soaked them in water and proceeded to plant them in eight-inch-deep holes that I had made in the receiving bed. Thus far, all by the book! Then a little topsoil mixed with manure was used to cover up the crowns and a little water sprinkled on top. So far, so good. The plantings were at least twelve inches apart; the annual, long-lived cultivars used were Purple and Jersey Series. As the tips grew out of the holes, I backfilled the dirt until by that first autumn, the former holes and bed were even-Steven. A mulch layer was put down on top and the bed rested for the winter. The following spring a few, but not all, thin asparagus stalks poked up and out of the berm. Again, they were a mix of female and male plants, and of two varieties. But not all of the plants grew. There were some barren spots that caused me great consternation. So, I bought a few more online and replanted them as needed. However, the ones that did sprout quickly grew in height. Like a doting dotard, I watched the progress daily and could almost taste the succulent stalks that were to come. It's as if I was cleverly grooming these innocent vegetables for a sinister purpose. But isn't most agriculture like that? Anyway, I finally achieved fairly

even growth from all the planted asparagus by the
end of the second season and let them fern out in late
summer for adequate root distribution. The
anticipation was killing me, but common gardening
wisdom suggested that by the third year the kid-
gloves could come off and I could raid that bed, slash
the penile-resembling protuberances, and boil up
some tasty treats. Yum, yum. Well, it kind of started
to happen the following May, however, not with the
vigorous panache that I had hoped. And to add to my
mental misery, the resident female snapping turtle
from our pond decided to crawl over three hundred
feet to lay her clutch of eggs right in the middle of the
asparagus bed. What was she thinking? What a
stinker. And what a muddy mess she made! Her deep
digging ruined, and even partially killed, a four-foot
section of asparagus. In addition, the rest of the plants
failed to live up to expectations. Sure, I was able to
harvest a few here and there, but not the bonanza I
had hoped for. Sadly, I leveled up the berm and stuck
back into place the multiple mangled and probably
dead asparagus crowns. Shortly after the baby turtles
hatched and made a beeline through the grass for the
pond – at least as fast as two-inch-long-reptiles can
crawl – I encircled the entire bed with staked and
ground-imbedded chicken wire so that during
ensuing years mama snapping turtle would think
twice before depositing her shelled progeny where

they did not belong. And it has worked thus far. The fencing was also a precautionary barrier to help prevent rude rabbits from diagonally snapping off new development. Anyhow, the turtle episode fucked me over as did the paltry production of asparagus. Now it was July and time to quit harvesting and let any new growth go to gigantic, four-foot-tall ferns with seeds. It was proper because the plants need to photosynthesize and keep expanding root-wise. Hopefully that would expand the root base and more plants would develop in the future thereby giving me more meals! But that did not happen. Ten years in, and my asparagus patch is patchy at best. There are some good years, but mostly bad. Granted we have had dry summers, however, all the extra watering, mulch applications and praying have gone for naught. Maybe I was praying to the wrong Gods? And wet summery conditions have also not helped. It's as if the asparagus plants have minds of their own and only cooperate on a whim. Still, I dutifully prune the enormous ferny growths every fall, add nutritious mulch as a top layer to the weeded bed and eternally hope for a better crop come next summer. What else can I do? I'm a sucker for homegrown asparagus, even if they clown on me and treat ME like an abject gardening failure.

29

Pole Beans?

Fuck the "Three Sisters" of indigenous lore. All the packages purchased at that certain big box home-improvement store had BUSH green beans plainly written on them. Blue Lake, Contender, and Tendergreen were the bought brands. They were ready to be planted right after a particular garden section was tilled, raked, and furrowed. It was that easy; what could go wrong? Hottie Blondie had her barefoot, barehanded, and Reiki-energized way of planting; the same "magical" techniques she utilized yearly which produced "tons" of luscious beans for our consumption. However, this year was different. One of the Three Sisters turned out to be exactly what the ancient Haudenosaunee tribes of modern New York State had intentionally planted, namely – pole beans! But I had expected bush beans. That's what the packs clearly read. I could still read and comprehend, I thought. WTF? I knew something was amiss by late June, when SOME of the fenced-in plants started to develop obvious tendrils that seemed to be searching for something to cling to. It appeared that every other growing bean plant - the ones remaining after repeated careful thinning of the properly spaced rows over a period of weeks - was a pole bean variety. How did that happen and what was I to do? It was a mixed-up and rapidly growing tangled jungle and I had to act fast. I had no time to complain at the store, to harbor resentments or any regrets. Remember, if you get lemons, make lemon meringue pie! So, I took it upon myself to hurriedly hammer some metal rebar posts into the ends of the seven rows and then strung different levels of nylon string between them lengthwise. Only upon completion of that temporary trellis did I explain the whole sordid situation to my puzzled wife. After all, she was the one who bought and meticulously inserted those dang seeds into the ground. I implored her to come outside and take a good hard look at those growing vegetables. She saw, she grimaced, and then she reluctantly accepted the fact that we were going to have more pole beans than bush beans. Such is life. But wait a gosh darn second, aren't pole beans just as good as bush beans? Well, in my opinion, yes and no. But I guess it also depends on what types of beans are purchased. Nonetheless, pole beans can be a pain in the ass to grow. Because of their wandering tendencies, they can quickly overwhelm a combination bean plot regardless of the trellising present. Because, as you may recall, I still had many bush plants present. What a potential disaster. However, dire circumstances were averted, and things worked out. Although initially I had to "train" the viny outgrowths to latch onto the horizontal stringing and purposely had to stop them from choking the lowly bush varieties at ground level. Of course, if I only had the pole types and no others, I would not have been concerned at all. In due course they would have "found" the lateral scaffolding and done their thing without any intervention from me. Oh well, I played bean policeman and managed to separate the two competitors as best as I could. And wouldn't you know it? The flat-sided pole beans became heavy producers while the bush ones were basically bush league. Whether they felt encroached upon is up to debate, however, our normally high-yielding bush assortments produced virtually diddly-squat. But how could I be disappointed when the "climbers" were magnificent? Daily pickings were required during July, August, and most of September just to alleviate the gravid build-up of beans. The quantity was great; the quality *menza menz*. The Blue Lake bush variety – which normally provides me with bucketfuls of tender, round, long green pods – are my favorite stringless beans. In my opinion, they taste much better than the "poles." To sum up, the pole beans that I was forced to reckon with that one season proved to be okay as far as flavor went and were devoured with relish. Not ketchup, only relish. The bush varieties stunk as far as yield was concerned that one fateful year, but hopefully will get it together for all future seasons. However, who can really tell if we will always be successful? The packages we continue to buy always say Bush Beans on them….

30

The Purple Menace

That title sounds so menacing, almost otherworldly. But, no, we are talking about the seldom grown purple raspberry, a long-lived staple in my stable of berry plants. However, it can be a real pain in the petunia to grow and manage. First and foremost are the fearsome quarter inch spikes that line the long vines that need to be trellised. Gloves and clothing often become unavoidably snagged on these stems, regardless of the care taken not to let that happen. Even the requisite protective plastic eyewear gets scratched now and again. However, sometimes I would rather work bare-armed in between the toothy branches and take my chances. A few cuts to my forearms are better than ripping apart cotton sleeves and cuffs. Summer management can be a hardship, but it is the fall where the bloodletting really gets flowing: there is the additional duty to prune out the old canes, which I had previously twisty-tied securely to the guide wire trellis contraption, and then to affix the new growth. Copious swearing is also involved when it comes time to cut and rip out the old and to make room for new growth for the following season. Another source of consternation is the tendency for the purple raspberry to try to implant its runners every autumn in a haphazard manner, away from the established row. I can't want that (I love saying that.)! Logically I wish to trellis the multitude of long, new vines along the built structure, but I also want to implant SOME of that new growth as well. But not all of it. I don't want a jungle with an overwhelming wall of non-yielding greenery. It's a tough balancing act - to anticipate great amounts of producing vines (primocanes) for the following year while keeping the current stock viable - by replanting a few runners as needed in the existing row. But the intentionally replanted runners are only a secondary source of continuity for the plants. The first being new growth which emanates every spring from the existing and established, multi-stemmed, root balls. The gardener-guided implantation process is easy: take the rooty-looking end of a runner that is already dragging itself in the dirt, dig a little shallow well in the weeded and mulched berm, stick in the end, cover with soil, and tamp in place (tip layering). The "new planting" will latch itself into the ground in a few weeks' time and hopefully start growing a new berry plant come next spring. However, that feat is not guaranteed to occur. Some of the implanted vines fail to grow and some do not mature into viable, fruit-producing canes. Fortunately, and as mentioned above, the mature bushes usually send up new growth year after year. But why even talk about such a seemingly vile and hard-to-raise raspberry plant? Well, for a two-to-three-week period beginning in the first week of July, my family and I are rewarded with what I personally consider to be the sweetest, juiciest, best-tasting berry there is. Period! We pick and pick the large, dark purple raspberries and relish the delectable flavor as we pop them in our mouths. While watching Wimbledon tennis matches on TV, we often bastardize the "Breakfast at Wimbledon" tradition of eating strawberries and cream by substituting our purple raspberries for the strawberries. Fortunately, and although they are out in the open, birds really don't bother them. Oh, there will be a peck mark here and there, but no wholesale robbery which occurs with exposed blueberry bushes. The purple berries come in a variety of sizes and purple-black colorations. The John Robertson cultivars I had originally planted are, like all "purple" varieties, a cross between black and red raspberry plants. But why did I plant these in the first place? I don't know; no one had suggested it. It had been an early experiment, just to see what would happen. A twenty-foot-long row was cleared of grass, prepared with mulch, and then ten bare-root sticklings were stuck into the dirt. Later, a metal-wire trellis was constructed when I realized that "purples" liked to "travel." These raspberries, although only yielding scrumptious berries for roughly a three-week period, are RELATIVELY easy to grow. However, the "pruning of the old" and "trellising and implanting of the new" every fall can be a slightly bloody and painful affair. But it is well worth it; an experiment that bears fruit to this day!

31

Huckleberries

Being called a huckleberry can be a term of derision – ala hapless Huckleberry Hound of yesteryear's cartoon world, or Mark Twain's happy-go-lucky literary protagonist, Huckleberry Finn. The word is also an old-fashioned expression of endearment (i.e., I want to be your huckleberry). My transplanted huckleberry bushes embody the latter. They were dug up as adults from my boyhood village in the Catskills, planted as a group in my new home's big backyard in 1992, and are still going strong. Although originally spaced five feet apart, and heavily pruned yearly, each woody huckleberry bush approaches 8 feet in height and at least 4 feet in diameter. And their substantial seasonal yields of small, dark blue berries have never waned nor wavered. But just what are these berries? Aren't they basically puny blueberries? No, they are not. The blueberry (genus Vaccinium) and huckleberry (genus Gaylussacia) are actually different plants. However, they are related and closely resemble each other. Bilberry, whortleberry, and hurtleberry were antiquated British names that linguistically morphed into "huckleberry" in colonial America. However, the two distinct families of "discovered" (of course, the indigenous North American tribes were

using and eating these berries for millennia) BLUE-
berry-yielding plants were often lumped together.
Hence, the confusion still exists to this day between
huckleberries and blueberries. In the Catskill region,
wild huckleberry shrubs are also known as bush
huckleberry and gopher-berry. They grew unattended
and unpicked – at least by people – in the unused
and overgrown pasture behind my childhood home.
As a pre-teen in the late summers of the early '70s, I
used to pass them by on many jaunts afield as a net-
wielding, amateur entomologist. I'd eat a few berries
here and there and then dash off in pursuit of flying
insects, etc. Not much thought was given to these
protruding woody bushes on the sloped, grassy,
former farm field. Close to twenty years later, five of
those large, familiar bushes now appeared in my new
home's back acreage, far from their original habitat.
Adult huckleberry plants are notoriously difficult to
grow, especially transplanted ones. I got lucky and all
five thrived and are still alive to this day, over three
decades since their involuntary abductions. Anyhow,
let's discuss blueberries (wild and cultivated) and
huckleberries and try to get to the nub of the
similarities and differences. Wild huckleberry picking
and eating is popular with humans, birds, and other
animals (especially Black bears), as is the harvesting of
naturally occurring low bush blueberry plants, such as
those found throughout the Adirondack mountains.

Although the yields of both uncultivated plants may be meager, it is a tasty hobby, nonetheless. Many was the time when my folks, sister, and I would dutifully trudge into the aforementioned abandoned field behind our house in late fall and collect our fill of wild huckleberries. They were similar in size and coloration to the high-altitude, wild, low-bush blueberries that my former girlfriend (now my wife) had much later introduced me to near her home in the Adirondacks. However, when it comes to flavor, the small huckleberries can be on the tart and bland sides whereas blueberries are of decent sweetness. Blueberry bushes grow fruit in large clusters whereas huckleberries are formed in smaller numbers. Blueberries are pale green or white on the inside, but huckleberries are either purple or dark blue when cut into. Huckleberries often have seeds that can sometimes be felt when eaten. Blueberries have soft seeds inside each delectable berry and are often undetectable. So, if blueberries are the princes, and huckleberries the paupers, why am I bothering to expound on my quintet of huckleberry bushes? Well, though I occasionally pop one or two into my pie-hole while brushing past them in late summer, they are mainly a decoy to keep birds away from my prized blueberry cultivars. Even though my blueberry bushes are securely fenced in, and with a protective netting on top, determined birds still find a way to get at them. Hence the huckleberry plants, to basically run interference. Oftentimes I will see scores of avian assholes – mainly catbirds, blue jays, black birds and crows – virtually "swimming" inside the huckleberry shrubs, all the while consuming the loss-leader berries. Better they nosh on the no-account huckleberries than on my treasured blueberries! Oftentimes, and at the end of the harvest season, the huckleberry plants will not have any remaining fruit on them. Nothing. Such is the nature of hungry birds that denude each plant down to the very last edible orb. I guess the huckleberry is popular and useful after all. It is also the state fruit of Idaho and Montana. So there!

32

The Blue Wave

That's how I refer to my fifty-plus blueberry bushes, although it could also mean a huge win for the Democratic party in any given election cycle. However, let's stick to the *politics* of raising and harvesting blueberries! Each and every bush is my horticultural pride and joy. Over the years I have carefully pruned and pampered them to get the largest possible yield of delicious and nutritious blueberries. And yet, some still don't produce regularly. Such is the finicky nature of blueberries and why I have so many shrubs. You never know when one will bite the dust or start to crump. Sometimes, the individual plant will appear leafy and robust, yet will be annoyingly devoid of berries when it counts. Anyway, to prevent an unplanned insurrection by an unexpected flash mob of birds, my ten or so original cultivars are surrounded by a six-foot tall, metal-staked, chicken wire enclosure with a detachable door and rolled-on, ½ inch-holed, bird-proof netting on top (the netting is rolled off every fall to prevent snow from crumpling the whole damn thing). All the moving pieces are held together with metallic hog ties. The metal stakes also have outside guide wires to prevent collapse when the top netting is placed during the summer. A casual reader may rightly ask as to why so much fuss and protection is needed. With such a perceived overabundance of plants, birds and other pesky animals should theoretically get their gullets stuffed while leaving more than enough for human consumption. Ha, ha. Not so fast bucko, not so fast! My extra sections of purposely uncovered huckleberry and blueberry bushes are virtually stripped of all fruit come the end of the season. And before I leveled up and decided to fully encase my additional fifty cultivars to help stop any future avian insurrections, I got very few berries from them. Sure, initially I tried using individual coverings like muslin cloth, scarecrows, motion detecting robotics, bitter bird spray that is applied to the berries, wind-moving chimes, and other "natural" products that were supposed to work. But they did not! Crows and blue jays are wily critters and found ways to get underneath the cheesecloth and muslin covers, and the bitterness of the berries did not bother them. Other birds, such as flycatchers, cat birds, sparrows and robins followed suit. Of course, on commercial berry farms (often called "barrens"), where there are acres and acres of bushes in the open, I'm sure the birds and other pests are not a serious threat. But in a suburban setting, with trees all around the berry patch, it's like shooting fish in a barrel. So, I got smart in a hurry, and although it was a strenuous project, the two structures barricading the blueberry bushes inside have lasted. Now I can get MY fill, year after year. However, I still have to replace rusted chicken wire sections here and there, and this is my second top covering in over two decades of outdoor usage. But that's not bad and it is so worth it. And now, a word or two about the blueberries. Finally, right? Because after rambling on about how much I love and protect them, let's discuss why that is. Even though mild maintenance is a must, and a wee bit of horticultural know-how for their general growth and well-being, I believe that no fruit is more rewarding to the gardener than the blueberry. Again, that's only my biased opinion. Besides exquisite flavor right off the bush, so to speak, the luscious berries are also full of anti-inflammatory nutrients such as ellagic acid, anthocyanins, and flavonoids. Vitamins C, K, and the mineral manganese are also plentiful per berry, besides small amounts of other nutraceuticals. Did I mention that they taste great? But I'm not alone. The U.S produces nearly 40% of the world supply of highbush blueberries. Somebody is eating them, consequently the crazy production numbers. There are always packages of them available in many large supermarkets regardless of the time of year. And even woodland creatures, including bears, chipmunks and rabbits, relish these tasty treats which are easy to pick and devour. Anyway, all blueberry plants need acidic soil to thrive. Early investigative botanists determined that blueberries grow best in very acidic, bog-like conditions, similar to cranberry habitats. A pH between 4 and 6 is considered ideal. And although I confess to NOT ever having tested my backyard dirt for acidity, I do create continuing favorable conditions for my blueberries. Each spring, not only does every bush get a handful of 10-10-10 fertilizer, but it also receives a handful of elemental sulfur. It may be overkill because ¾ pound of sulfur is usually adequate to profoundly acidify 100 square feet of garden area. However, my sandy-loam soil readily absorbs it, and the plants seem to love this yearly treatment. Next on my list is to keep the ground underneath the blueberry plants, which are rather shallow rooted, clear of grass and weeds. This is done for esthetics (I like things very neat and clean, in case you haven't figured that out yet!) and for maximum absorption of water and nutrients by each plant. But instead of using potentially toxic Roundup, I apply sprayed-on 30% vinegar to tamp down the undesirable green growth (obviously it does not work as well as potent commercial herbicides, but it sort of does the job) before and after the berry growing season - never during. Some people mulch the plants with acidy pine bark or even pine needles to help keep the moisture close to the roots and the pH low. I don't. And speaking of water, blueberries absolutely love it. The more the better. Soggy, boggy and foggy conditions make them thrive. Of course, they don't like to stand in flooded terrain, but steady moisture is a must for generous berry seasons. The shrubs can survive drought, though. However, the resultant overall yield, and the berries themselves, will often be undersized. Sometimes there will be a dry spell and then a deluge of rainwater. That is bad, too. It can cause the ripening berries to crack open because of the sudden increase and uptake of water. Those split berries can become readily infected, mushy, and non-consumable - at least by humans. Additionally, sudden heat stress can cause wrinkling of the berries. If that is rapidly followed by an influx of water, cracking of the skin occurs, making the berries inedible. And now a word about diseases. The UNaffected plant has vibrant oblong, slightly glossy, green leaves with no holes or discolorations in them. The ripened, plump, unblemished dark blue berries are covered with a fine layer of a silvery-white substance called the "bloom." All normal. However, Mummy Berry disease (fungus) and a host of viruses that cause leaf-wilting and brown spots (rust) can wreck a blueberry patch. Nevertheless, most cultivars that are commercially purchased have been bred to withstand the majority of viral, bacterial, and fungal attacks. Ensuing wilt, yellowed leaves, and other such telltale symptoms of "illness" can actually be signs of poor growing conditions and not representative of the plant itself. Even so, there are a few things that can still affect blueberries, and cold temps are usually not one of them. Speaking of chill, even repetitive and harsh Canadian winters don't seem to flummox the northern-bred cultivars. Anyway, back to the obvious external attacks: yellow-necked caterpillars can skeletonize the foliage of a blueberry bush in a hurry and "hurt" the entire plant. The affected branches look like a giant, silken mass with eaten leaves mixed in with wriggling caterpillars. It loosely resembles the tent caterpillar infestations of deciduous trees. The larvae pupate in the ground, turn into brown moths, and start the process all over again in the spring. Attention must be paid, and the blueberry plants observed at regular intervals for this affectation not to get out of hand. Whenever I spot it happening on one or two shrubs, I cut off the damaged branches and dispose of the larvae and mutilated stems. That usually solves the problem until the following year. Oh, well. Next up are galls. They are the natural reactions and woody outgrowths of a plant desperately trying to wall its sensitive tissues off from a noxious substance or invader. They may become readily noticeable on branches after the last of the leaves have fallen off in late autumn. The galls can approach two to three inches in size and appear as distinctive, "kidney-shaped," mini-oblong footballs encasing a live stem. Multiple appalling galls can appear on one or many blueberry plants and, although not deadly to the bush, can be a source of poor yields if not dealt with promptly. And believe it or not, they are caused by a miniature flying insect called the Blueberry Stem Gall wasp. Yes, a six-legged and teeny-weeny winged "bug" is the cause of all this unhealthy and unesthetic bulbous bullshit. The miniscule larvae of this wasp are the actual guilty parties. They induce the blueberry branches, where the eggs are laid, into overprotective overreactions, thus the galls. Cutting into one in the fall reveals the many chambers of the wormy tenants and their upcoming pupation. They emerge from small holes in the spring as fully formed adults and start the process all over again. But getting rid of these problematic tenants is as easy as cutting off the affected stem/ branch and destroying the galls before winter sets in. However, if holes are noticed in the galls in the spring, it is too late because the hatched wasps have flown the coop. Pesticides are ineffective against these native pests; physical pruning works best. To date, I have only had one year where there was a veritable infestation of my blueberry plants. I swore, pruned, swore, and pruned some more. In the end, all the highly visible galls were removed, burned, and order was restored to the berry patches. And I have not had a repeat performance since. I'm not sure why, because the wasps are endemic species and recur every year. Nevertheless, I am always on the lookout for those nasty-looking branch-bunions. Okay, so blueberries aren't as easy to raise as I seemingly alluded. So why did I plant them in the first place? Well, mainly because of my love of most berries. And, even though I already had the wild huckleberries in place, I still had plenty of backyard space available for more fruit-bearing flora. But this time they were store-bought and would hopefully give me store-quality berries, or better. I was secretly hoping for better. I ordered ten plants online from a nursery in Michigan that had a good reputation for selling cold-hardened blueberry plants, ones that would grow in my zone. Originally planted in a rectangular pattern, in a previously cleared and mowed meadow, the ten three-year old cultivars were spaced 5-6 feet apart and consisted of Jersey, Blue-Ray, Herbert, Coville, and Chandler varieties. Since blueberries reproduce best by cross-pollination between differing cultivars – accomplished by wind, bees, and wasps – I was all set. There were no concerns about wild animals devastating the youngling plants. Also, there were no concerns about growing conditions, either. In other words, there were no worries at all. I cavalierly and naïvely measured and then stuck the green-stemmed plants into the dirt in the springtime and literally walked away. And wouldn't you know it? All the baby bushes matured rather quickly, nothing demolished them, and within a few short years grew into the plants I still have to this day. It's as if the deer, rabbits, birds, insects, viruses, bacteria, and fungi did not get the inceptive memo about the "free" and succulent meals available to them until it was too late to ruin a good thing. But today, every *bloody* animal and disease knows about them. And, as stated at the beginning, without barrier protection and circumspection, there would be blighted, chewed, and destroyed blueberry plants, and very few berries. I subsequently ordered and planted forty more bushes in a large square next to the first "experimental" bunch because I wasn't sure if I would get any berries from the ten already growing. These forty included additional varieties such as Blue-Crop, Patriot, Berkley, and Northern. The various types of blueberry plants ripened at succeeding stages during the summer. Jerseys and Covilles were early, the Patriots were later on, and so forth. It felt great walking among the many plantings and watching them grow up. As they grew into their woody, branched selves, and after multiple failed attempts at dissuading dastardly birds and mammals from dining on them, I set up the previously mentioned barriers around them. When pruning in November, I top off each plant so that it remains no taller than 5 feet. In addition, and most importantly, I make sure each bush has two to three old stems and two to three young ones. As the old ones eventually die, the previous new growth replaces them. However, if the plant is left alone to grow "wild," with huge amounts of branches and stems, the yields frequently go down. So, judicious pruning is a must if you want the most fruit from a limited number of blueberry shrubs. And, as stated before, not all the plants produce every year. Some take a vacation without telling me ahead of time. It happens. Late-summer eating is straightforward and natural. But for winter consumption, my wife evenly spreads the summer-picked and unwashed (washing ruins them quickly if not eaten promptly) berries on wax paper-lined cookie sheets and pops them into the freezer. After the berries are thoroughly frozen, she fills dozens and dozens of large Ziploc bags and returns them to the freezer. It's that easy. This way, her morning cereal flakes can have "summer goodness" sprinkled on them all winter long. And there are plenty to bake with, too. The unfrozen previously frozen blueberries do not quite have the same fresh taste, but they are still more flavorful than store-bought ones. Speaking of flavor, EACH blueberry plant's berries, and regardless of the cultivar, have their own unique size, aroma, and taste. And that can change from year to year. It is a strange phenomenon. Of course, we treat our plants as individuals and get to know them very well. When having friends over during berry-harvesting season, I recommend them to try a few ripe ones from different bushes, decide which ones are sweetly palatable, and then encourage them to thoroughly pick that bush. Keeping the grass mowed inside the two enclosures, with a push mower no less, can be backbreaking. But the tidy-looking result is well worth it. I'm always grateful for the "all organic" yearly abundance they bestow upon me and my family. In summary, during most late summers, stepping back and gazing upon the blue wave of ripe blueberries is a sight to behold. And then I notice my wife coming out of the house wearing a very skimpy bikini, a large-brimmed, sun-proof hat and holding two large, empty colanders as well as a portable, fold-out chair. She is on her way to the enclosures to pick blueberries and get some sunny epidermal exposure at the same time - and yet another titillating sight to behold. Bonus!

33

Golden Jewels

Most visitors, including some curious animals, are probably surprised to see a neatly trimmed hedgerow of golden-hued raspberries growing in my big backyard. But then, why not? I love to eat all kinds of edible berries; what can I say? Plus, one of my dirty little secrets is that I miserably tanked while attempting to grow traditional red raspberries. But boy did I try. Many growing seasons were wasted during my futile venture to raise those crimson raspberries. I tried VARIOUS types from VARIOUS greenhouses, and at VARIOUS cultivar ages, and planted them at VARIOUS times of the year. Nothing doing. However, the succeeding golden raspberries seemed to like my act and responded positively to my gardening overtures. But why? They are supposedly similar to the red raspberry family, but without the anthocyanin pigmentation. WTF? Anyway, after I had cleared out the last of my failed reds, I hand-tilled the row of soil and prepared the bed as best as I could. A little fertilizer, a little manure mulch… you know, anything to help. And then I purposely mixed-up and planted two types of foot-high, everbearing, golden raspberry stalks (Golden Harvest and Honey Queen) which I had ordered online from a nursery in Wisconsin. One variety was an early producer while the other was a late summer and fall cultivar. But what did I know? My childhood experience consisted of interacting with bountiful, trellised, Heritage Everbearing and Latham Reds which were in a large, carefully curated (thanks to Grandpa Pete) patch next to my family's huge garden. As a young lad I had learned the basics and knew about primocanes, namely, that new shoots produced berries the following year while the old ones would die back after their current crop. I assumed the same for the yellow ones that I had newly planted at my own home. And I was right. Planted one foot apart, they all took, and I was beyond pleased. And they quickly jumbled together; I could not discern which were which. The early-bearing ones looked similar to the late-bearing ones. Oh, well. It was all my fault and now I had to live with it or start over. I decided to live and let live. Both types of mellow yellows, as I like to call them, are a delight to grow and eat. I use the word mellow because the flavor is not as bold as the red raspberries' and can be rather bland, especially during prolonged wet weather conditions when excess water is taken up by the plants. The yellow early-yielding variety is slightly richer in taste compared to the later one, whose berries tend to be rather flavorless. Okay, some fun facts and personal tales about these raspberries. Firstly, stink bugs love to crawl among the jagged leaves of these plants! These six-legged skunks are true bugs and sip juices from the raspberry stems through their sharp beaks. But they don't do any real harm, unless there is an infestation of these bugs. The adult berries can sometimes be coated and dotted with orange-colored, mildew-like growth. Since I don't use any commercial herbicides, pesticides or fungicides on any of my veggies or fruiting plants, I have always assumed that this localized berry discoloration is normal. And I have also assumed that they are safe to eat. I'm still here, so…. Weeding the raspberry patch periodically throughout the summer months is important. After both new and old canes are cut back to 1 foot tall every November, any remaining old, loose, withered, and obviously dead canes are also removed. And the area is weeded once more before winter sets in. Some growers will prune the spent growth as well as next season's primocanes down to ground level. It's a personal choice. In the spring, raspberries are one of the first plants to develop and quickly overwhelm any rogue plants that wish to compete with them. Even so, vines and undesirable undergrowth are best removed to give the raspberries a good start against any weedy invaders. Because red and yellow raspberries spread and propagate through underground rhizomes (runners), new growths are frequently spotted in the grass near the original twenty-foot-long by two-foot-wide row. These pop-ups can be dug up and used as new plantings or just mowed over, to help preserve the vigor of the original plants. And although raspberry canes usually have a life expectancy of two decades, mine have been going at it for over twenty-five years. The slightly prickly plant stems can get very lanky and then flop downward due to the heaviness of the berry load. Room must be left on either side of the row for the arching canes or, alternatively, trellises can be constructed to mitigate the overflowing greenery and clumps of yellow treats. I have found that yellow raspberries are not as well received by family members, as compared to purple raspberries and blueberries. Friable and easily spoiled, even when kept in a refrigerator after picking, these fragile berries are best eaten fresh and right away. Though definitely not tart and acidy like their red counterparts, I would also not consider yellow raspberries as sweet. Banal and free of "bad" flavor would be more descriptive terms. They are relatively hardy and can be harvested into late September. At the very least they provide quirky and eccentric accents to any fruit-growing endeavors and colorful garnishes to fruit salads.

34

The "Fall Boys"

Maturing fruits and veggies have an internal biologic clock that is influenced and modified by inclement weather conditions, water availability, ambient sunshine, pests, heat, humidity, and luck. Most berries and green produce are gathered at certain times during late summer and very early fall, all based on those above-mentioned considerations. Buzzing cicadas and Monarch butterflies herald the coming of autumn in my homely hamlet just as I harvest the last of my beans and yellow squash. With that, the "gardening season" is essentially over. It can be a bittersweet time. Withered and spent plant-stems are pulled out and discarded, and the persnickety and pernicious weeds finally realize that their time is up too. Moving into late October and a dreary serenity descends on that previously productive plot of soil. In short order Jack Frost will come a-calling to finish off what's left. But wait, what IS left? Yes, the three cold-hardy "fall boys" are still going strong, as long as there is no early freeze in sight. Beets, Swiss chard and Japanese eggplants are the hard-nosed citizens of my veggie garden and are mostly impervious to bad growing conditions, hungry mammals, insects, and chilly atmospheric conditions. Of course, early on they still need to be cared for, weeded, watered, thinned, and fenced in, but then they take it from there and become less finicky than other edible plants. And they selflessly keep on giving me "farm to table" food right up until their respective, bitter-cold demises. Swiss chard, supposedly named because of ancient Swiss and French connections, are relatively big garden plants (up to three feet tall), with thick angular stalks and large veined, deeply wrinkled (like a human male scrotum when it's cold), leafy blades. The leaf blade can be red or green; the stems are usually white, yellow, green or red. This nutritious and mineral-laden vegetable is related to the beet and there can be some confusion when talking about its speciation and scientific nomenclature. However, one glance at it and a seasoned gardener instantly knows that it is chard and not beet! It is a favorite of mine because virtually no animal, including slugs, is fond of the MATURE plant (I have to qualify that last statement because rabbits DO like to nibble down the young seedlings, and a fence is most beneficial for their initial survival). Occasionally there will be a hole here and there, but overall, no insecticides are needed to thwart unwanted pests from feasting on fully developed chard. And it grows prolifically, yielding a delicious addition to main meals or as its own, standalone serving. A large pot of cut up leaves and stems boil down to a hearty portion of a nutty-flavored veggie that needs just a little Kerrygold butter and salt for a great meal. As the summer progresses into late fall it is still growing, with magnificent foliage casting shadows in its row preventing weed propagation. For the uninitiated, and from a distance, it vaguely resembles bok choy on steroids! Harvesting Swiss chard is quick and easy. Parts of the plant can be sectioned at any time and boiled for a yummy dish or eaten raw as part of salads and wraps. Just to add, sauteed and cooked chard is less bitter than fresh. And to think that a plant so big and bountiful started out as teeny-tiny, black seeds with resultant puny sprouts that needed to be weeded, thinned and protected. And then - boom, a virtual bonanza of beautiful green and red leaves festooning the planted rows, ready to be consumed at any time. Beets, beets, beets…. Of worldwide distribution, I grew up eating European borscht (beet soup) as a kid and appreciate beets' unique coloration and flavor. And most vegetable gardens would not be "complete" without at least a few rows of planted beets, or beetroots, if referring to their proper British name. It is also known as the table beet, garden beet, red beet, dinner beet, or golden beet. The entire plant can be consumed, leaves and all, but the bulbous taproot is the "business end" of this unique vegetable. There are many recognized cultivars of the same species of beet including the sugar beet and mangelwurzel. In other words, beets and their related subspecies and cultivars are variations on the same theme. Of ancient lineage, beets were originally cultivated in the Middle East for their leaves, then by the Romans for their roots. During that time-period in history, many human ailments were treated with beet juice. It was also used as a dye for wines and other products that required a red coloration. Most modern nations have even incorporated the beet into unique, country-specific cuisine such as Ukrainian borscht, Australian pickled beets, Polish *chrain* condiment, Lithuanian beetroot soup, Serbian beetroot salad, Indian spiced beetroot, German mashed beetroot, etc. This peeled vegetable can be sliced, diced, steamed, boiled, roasted, and pickled. It can be essentially "mangled" and still produces a delicious and savory meal or garnish. And its spinach-like leaves can be added to salads or eaten as is. Beets have a fair amount of nutritional value and there is some evidence of the juice having positive effects on the reduction of systolic blood pressure. And of course, the signature red color betanin is not broken down by the body and is excreted in urine and feces, coloring those excrements on the way out. The more beets that are devoured, the redder the bodily waste becomes. Beets are fairly easy to grow, but can be attacked by meadow voles, those mouse-like pests of lawns and gardens. You know, the short-tailed, shrew-like mammals that resemble furry bullets and run in a straight line when hurriedly crossing a roadway. Yes, those critters. Once they get into a row of beets, watch out. They absolutely love them and will gouge out huge sections of the root balls thereby ruining them for human consumption. Because they are so small, effective fencing to keep them out is difficult to achieve. Telltale markings, which include shallow holes and zigzagging surface furrows, showcase the presence of voles (moles are carnivorous and not a threat to gardens). Trapping and rodent repellents are recommended for their eventual ouster. However, I have usually lost the battle when their invasion is heavy. Some growing seasons are better than others but be prepared for beet loss thanks to these hungry and most unwanted little buggers. Therefore, plant more beets! Eggplants are the final members of this trio of cold-defying vegetables. They are popular foods; what American hasn't heard of eggplant parmesan? Anyway, like tomatoes and white potatoes, eggplant varieties fall into the nightshade family: their leaves and stems are poisonous and can make you sick. Belladonna, tobacco (nicotine poisoning), and mandrake are also members of this diffuse plant family and are considered deadly. But the low hanging and colorful eggplant produce is a delight to grow and eat. The contents of the globes are described as meaty, fleshy and seedy. And the shapes of the veggies can be round, football-shaped (oblong), as well as elongated and tapered at one or both ends. Some even have a vaguely phallic appearance. The hue-inspired designations can range from Great White to Deep Purple, just like the names of two of my favorite rock bands. Like ornamental gourds, these veggies can also be vertically striped, as well! The traditional, thick-skinned, purple, ovoid (globe) eggplant is a staple of most restaurant menus and homemade meals. This is the one most often sold in grocery stores, too. The Italian eggplants are smaller and sweeter versions of the above and the innards more tender. The Japanese eggplant – my favorite and the only one I grow – has the best taste, outer texture, and thinnest skin of the three. They are long and thin, sometimes reaching a foot in length. A shiny magenta, they keep on yielding until a super-deep frost occurs. The dark green leafy plants, with purplish stems, can grow to nearly three feet tall and are resistant to most mammalian and arthropod attacks. But why tempt fate or furry foes? I always put a chicken wire fence around the newly growing eggplant seedlings so as not to entice rogue rabbits or wayward woodchucks who may happen to come sauntering by looking for tender plants to snack on. And it works. In no time flat, the Japanese eggplants are sturdy and mature plants, ready to yield fantastic results. Besides my wife making the obligatory parmesan, often I simply like to bake the eggplants, slit them lengthwise, and scoop out the pale, soft insides for a great veggie dinner. The seeds are soft, palatable, and not an issue. Add a little topping condiment of mayo mixed with soy sauce and each bite of the tender eggplant becomes a culinary delight.

35

Window Dressing

Surrounding our charming property, in dribs and drabs, are multiple flower beds, arborvitae, Blue Spruce trees, prickly barbary shrubs, Privet bushes, and day lilies - not to mention the scores of other intentionally planted plants that dot the interior of our big backyard. Those include a dogwood tree, lilac bushes, rhododendrons, shrubby potentilla, and more flowers. With all this extraneous yearly growth and extensive lawn to manage, it's no wonder that SOME people hire professional landscapers and gardeners to do the dirty work. How many times has Hottie Blondie turned to me in bewilderment and said, "YOU wanted and created all of this. And if you and I can't handle it, then we'll hire someone!" Truer words were never spoken so often, darn it. But, alas, we are still "handling" it, even though age and infirmity are slowly creeping up on us both. I mean, my wife has already pared down her herb garden and no longer plants ornamental vegetation indiscriminately. However, it would be difficult to part with the current encircling beauty that effortlessly brings needed gladness to our eyes and souls. So, we lace up our sturdy Merrells (or go barefoot as my wife often does), don our gay apparel, and venture forth on most spring, summer, and fall days to tend to our garden, fruit trees, lawn, shrubbery, conifers, and numerous flowers. Fellow gardeners will feel our "pain." It's a constant watchfulness of sorts and cyclical in nature. Both annuals and perennials need to be looked after based on seasonal schedules. You know, tulip, crocus, and daffodil bulb-planting in the fall, even though they are perennials and will most likely keep on popping up every spring. The back-of-the-property, nursery-bought, and thirty-year old blue spruces resemble a giant hedgerow, towering over the native trees. Though some have browned near the bottoms, all are still kicking! The front of our place has sporadic patches of planted day lilies, the ones with thick green stems and bright, orange blossoms. They are a harbinger of early summer, and together with richly hued irises, lend much needed coloration to a green and mostly grassy environment. A solitary American red maple tree graces the very middle of the yard, with its huge, dorsally dark red and ventrally green leaves. The lone orange blossom plant and tall lilac bushes give off wonderful sights and scents in late spring. My wife will often bring the freshly picked cuttings indoors for a fragrant, olfactory treat. Finally, most of this "unnecessary" flora that virtually rings our acreage is regularly mulched and kept weed-free for our esthetic pleasure. Though not the Hanging

Gardens of Babylon, at least we take good care of what we have and are proud to live among our many and varied oxygen and food-producing "pals."

Seasons

My favorite season? Fall. This old timer's birthday is in October. You know, the month with a popular and widely "celebrated" holiday that does not have an official day off: Halloween. In addition, most plants in the northeastern U.S. start to die by late autumn, or at least they go into their respective winter slumbers. Summer is blissfully over, and I am no longer suffering from gardening "aggravation saturation." Thank God! Amen! But seriously, it's the end of the book and I am extremely grateful to the readers who have indulged my carping about horticulture. But why am I like this? Who likes to listen to a bitter old prick endlessly complain about things he was mostly responsible for? Nobody, not even Hottie Blondie or my cats! Perhaps it is my innate and psychological pain body (according to that New Age huckster Eckhart Tolle) coming to the fore and dominating my personality? Is that it? Do I whine in fervent hope of better results or for an occasional "atta boy"? Am I also starved for emotional placation due to perceived slights from dumb animals and innocent-looking fruits and vegetables? Wow, too *heavy* man! Anyway, thank you for putting up with the rancid ramblings of a dodgy codger in the twilight of life.

Last Words

I drink lots of warm V-8 juice, mainly the low-salt variety, and I eat most vegetables. Does that make me a photosynthetic-lifeform lover or hater? Am I a paragon of vegan virtue or merely a merciless and feckless vegetarian engaging in the wholesale slaughter and consumption of fruits and veggies? Most likely the latter…. Seriously though, I'm no vegan. I tend to identify as someone who eats fruits, vegetables AND real meat. But I do groom palatable young plants and berries just so I can prey on them later. Yikes, say it ain't so! It sounds so horrible, premeditated, and inappropriate. Alas, manmade agriculture was meant to function this way because humans need to eat, too. "Oh, bother," as Winnie the Pooh would often say. Anyway, those above-mentioned, emotion-ladened sentiments about horticulture are a part of my ongoing gardening journey (i.e., one that is frequently filled with psychological loathing of the growing process yet juxtaposed with the anticipatory excitement of the harvest phase). A true love/hate relationship with living, edible vegetation.

Thanks for the read.

About the Author

Dr. I. Mayputz (not his real name) graduated with highest honors from high school, pharmacy college and summa cum laude from dental school. After completing a master's degree in prosthodontics at a then prestigious institution, he embarked on his dental career in private practice. He is now retired. As an elite Master's athlete, he has won various championships in singles tennis, sprinting, snowshoe racing, javelin and singles pickleball. In addition to being a verbal artist, Reiki Master, certified Master Gardener, naturalist and part-time naturist, he is also known as a caustic wit and provocateur. Dr. I. Mayputz has previously published comedy novels using his pseudonym as well as released numerous nature articles in regional journals under his real name. Additionally, he has authored multiple scholarly pharmaceutical and dental abstracts and written many children's books, also under his given name. Lastly, he wrote this book to entertain family, old friends, fellow gardeners and any curious sod willing to vicariously *experience* the "joy" of planting and growing things.

For more alleged levity by Dr. I. Mayputz, please read:
Dental School: A Bizarre Comedy
Pharmacy College: Crazy Daze and Hazy Nites
Elementary School: Wits and Twits
Junior High: The Muddle Years
High School: Buffoonery Central
Dental Delirium: A "Humorous" Look at Dentistry
Retired... And I'm Still Tired!
Drugstore Delirium: A "Humorous" Look at Retail Pharmacy
Pickleball is a Priority!

WHO
DAT?